DATE DUE

1976: Agenda for Tomorrow

Also by Stewart L. Udall

The Quiet Crisis

STEWART L. UDALL

1976:
AGENDA
FOR
TOMORROW

HARCOURT, BRACE & WORLD, INC.

NEW YORK

FOR

Tom, Scott, Lynn
Lori, Denis, and James
—and their generation

May they deal gently with the
world—and it with them.

Foreword

The Quiet Crisis, published in 1963, was largely a work of
historical interpretation. In the spirit of the classic mission
of the Department of the Interior, and on behalf of the
future, I had originally intended to follow it with a book
that would outline needed conservation plans and programs designed to reduce and then eliminate the continuing blight of the national estate. After much thought and
several false starts, however, I did not write that book,
because I came to see that the total-environment approach
of "the new conservation" demanded concepts large
enough to relate conservation to the overriding issues of
our age. You cannot, in short, save the land unless you save

the people. True conservation, moreover, begins wherever the people are and with whatever trouble they are in.

More and more it seemed to me that the growing crusade for conservation would become a fringe movement, a marginal activity helplessly witnessing the slow erosion of its own values, unless its activities and outlook were related to the questions whose answers would, in fact, determine the habitat of man in the United States. I began to perceive that if the ultimate objective of conservation was the preservation of a life-giving milieu for man, then wise conservationists would be compelled to develop an ecology of man that would mesh with the forces already shaping the American future.

Consequently, it became clear to me that a meaningful agenda for tomorrow would evolve not from a specialized approach to the over-all environment, but from an attempt to achieve a full picture of the interrelated elements of American life. Thus this writing task became a struggle to understand our contemporary civilization—and therefore it increasingly leaned on the judgments of individuals who were also struggling to see American life with open eyes. Such seeing is hard to come by, because it means trying to see without blinkered preconceptions. If it works, however, there is vision.

In addition to my wife, Lee, I am deeply indebted for insights and criticisms provided by these friends who reviewed certain chapters: James McGregor Burns, Charles F. Schultze, Charles Haar, Ernest Lefever, Charles F. Luce, Lawrence Halprin, my brother, Representative Morris K. Udall, and my Interior Department colleagues David S. Black, Stanley A. Cain, Milner B. Schaefer, and Fred Singer. In addition, I owe a special debt to Henry S. Bloomgarden and John McGinty, who assisted me in the assembly and preparation of the materials for this book. Their ideas, insights, and capacity for provocative dialogue—and similar contributions by my editor, William B. Goodman—made the writing of this book an exciting intellectual exercise.

STEWART L. UDALL

WASHINGTON, D.C.
JULY, 1968

Contents

Introduction

All sophistication comes full circle: first untutored simplicity, then complexity, and later a more sophisticated
(and complex) return to simplicity; first, the natural, then
the artificial, and then a sophisticated return to the natural.
Antaeus, the mythical giant, could not be defeated in
wrestling as long as he remained in contact with the earth.
It is a lesson for modern man. He severs the ties with
nature at his peril.

One discovers in Stewart Udall's writing, as in the
writings of all the greatest conservationists, that he is not
talking just about the land, about natural resources, about
plants and animals. He is talking about human values, and

about a view of nature and man's place in it that merits the attention of any thoughtful modern. He argues for man as a nurturing rather than a destroying creature— for humans not cooped up, dulled, and alienated, but in touch with the land and living things, reverent, healing, renewing, committed to preserve, to enhance, to enjoy. It is a view close to nature, yet a highly civilized view.

But it has been clear for some time that Stewart Udall was moving beyond the classic conservationist role. During his eight years as the Secretary of the Interior he acted consistently to broaden the concepts of conservation. Increasingly, he has dealt with issues in the context of their relationships to our entire society. His wide-ranging interests and curiosities, his broad personal and public experience of our national life, his inclination to deal with causes rather than symptoms drew him inevitably toward a diagnosis of our total problem.

I wish every American would read and reflect on Chapter 5 of the book. In this chapter Mr. Udall proposes a set of challenges for the nation that would lift us out of our present urban and racial difficulties and on toward a future worthy of our great beginnings. The imminence of 1976, the two hundredth anniversary of our independence, leads him to call it Project 76.

It is a valid vision. It cannot be said too often that the tensions and disaffections that plague this nation today will not be cured by a punitive effort to control negative attitudes and actions. A policy built on fear and hostility will reap the whirlwind. The only possible cure lies in a great new burst of constructive, affirmative action to solve our problems. And that will come only in response to goals that excite the imagination of the American people, in response to a new vision of where we are going as a nation. Stewart Udall has such a vision, and his concluding chapters suggest no vagueness as to its implementation. Here he plunges with vigor and understanding into unavoidable yet frequently ignored issues: politics, population, and the manner of life we want—and can achieve. In fact, he tells us—and I think we should listen—how to bring about the total renewal of our cities and the nation.

The challenge for the remainder of this century is to make ours a livable society in every sense of the word, a society that reveres life, honors the individual, and places humane values at the top of the agenda. Stewart Udall, through this book, will help to guide us in our response to that challenge.

JOHN W. GARDNER

WASHINGTON, D.C.
JULY, 1968

1976: Agenda for Tomorrow

Prologue

One cannot survey the American scene today, or contemplate our future, without feelings of acute ambivalence. The performance of our economic system, the successes of our science and technology, the promise of improved education, the creative ferment among the young—all this quickens our hopes. Yet we are dismayed by the failures and forces that dehumanize and defeat the finest dreams and plans of this generation. Nothing dishonors us more, or does more to delimit the possibilities of genuine progress, than the flaws that cause us to misunderstand the legacy of the past and misuse the opportunities of today.

It is the waste that appalls us most. The waste that

allows madmen to destroy the lives of our most promising leaders; the waste of the human potential of the Indian, the Negro, and the "permanent" poor (who could do so much to enrich our national life if they were only given a chance) ; the waste of affluence through misdirection; the waste of the beauty and order and cleanliness of the land, and, above all, the waste of a clear and present opportunity to build, on this continent and in this country, a civilization that could make us, once again, "the last, best hope of earth."

This book—though it represents reflections of public service under two Presidents over an eight-year period—has been finished during the rush of turbulent, tragic events. The assassinations of Dr. Martin Luther King, Jr., and Senator Robert F. Kennedy, the unparalleled political decisions of the spring of 1968, the burning and disorders in the nation's capital and other major cities, the blunt indictment of our social attitudes and institutions by the Kerner Commission were the sober backdrop for this book. I wrote remembering arson smoke curling high over the low Washington sky line, the cruel subtraction of hope one felt as the gallant and idealistic life of Robert Kennedy ebbed away in a few sorrowful hours, the humiliation one felt as the finest American Negro leader of this century was destroyed by the very violence he abhorred. (Had he not, for his devotion to the principles of nonviolence, won the world's most respected prize for the promotion of peace?)

There was also a vivid recollection of the solemn warning served upon the citizens of a great industrial state by a governor who declared that its cities were "slowly dying"; the verdict of an itinerant British journalist that "the American landscape is visible graveyard of all our misconceptions about city planning, individual liberty and free enterprise"; and the thoughtful look of a Texas mayor

4

as he noted that his city had eight times as many gun homicides in 1967 as *all* of Great Britain.

There is today a silent but profoundly significant competition in this country between humanizing, life-expanding forces and blind forces that are demeaning and defeating life.

This is the book of an optimist who believes we can identify these forces, control them, and find our way through and beyond the disordered priorities and outdated institutions that now confuse our national purpose. It is a search for an agenda for tomorrow—an agenda capable of restoring a vision, of reframing an American dream powerful enough to enlist our minds and persuasive enough to revive our ancient faith in the future of our country.

I

1. 1945-1968:
The Distorted Years

"The truth, the central stupendous truth, about developed countries today is that they can have—in anything but the shortest run—the kind and scale of resources they decide to have. . . . It is no longer resources that limit decisions. It is the decision that makes the resources. This is the fundamental revolutionary change—perhaps the most revolutionary mankind has ever known." —U THANT

Were a panel of historians asked to evaluate the last one hundred years of our history, it might well rate our achievements in science and engineering, in economic expansion, and in innovative politics and social welfare as extraordinary. It is equally probable that our failure to achieve the balanced pattern of growth that is the hallmark of a genuine civilization would be identified as the main American weakness.

The Old Adam of excessive individualism, with all its strengths and serious flaws, marred this country's advance during the unfolding of the Industrial Revolution. Our own time is an even more telling case study of uneven

9

growth. No period since the founding years of the republic has been more creative—and destructive; more filled with climactic accomplishments—and more frustrating to human aspirations.

In the immediate aftermath of a great war, nations, whether defeated or victorious, are susceptible to crystallizing influences which may set a cycle for a whole generation. Our own experience shows that our current beliefs about world order and domestic priorities crystallized at the end of World War II. High tides of history washed over us in the spring and summer of 1945: Hitler was dead; Churchill was out of power; a new international organization—the United Nations—was created. In a matter of months the American people found themselves with a new President, with military victories over Germany and Japan, and with a new weapon capable of obliterating life on the entire planet. The sudden sobriety resulting from the nuclear bombing of Hiroshima foretold the turbulence and tension of a new order being born. That much was certain.

At home, demobilization and reconversion occurred in a house with two windows: one faced outward to the chaos and hopes of a new world; the other, to the inner courtyard of our national life. This was the setting in which our personal goals and ideas of national progress were formed. The learned and unlearned lessons of the past, the war-end expectations, the backward pull of race prejudice, the tug of outdated institutions, the unachieved ambitions of the Depression years all helped determine the options open to the American mind. The mood that followed the swift sequence of events alternated between weariness and ebullience. But the heritage of hyperindividualism quickly emasculated the spirit of co-operation that had won the war, and inclined us to be impatient with planning or

10

anything but minimal talk of new national goals. The welter of mixed emotions and confused aims blurred our vision and made us put primary trust in our prowess. Had we not won the war, achieved "impossible" feats of production, and made the atom bomb as well? Thus primed, we fell back on the pragmatic instincts that throughout so much of our history had served us so well.

Up to a point, the old first-things-first policy paid off. In defense, in world diplomacy, in redirecting the economy to consumer goods we did extremely well. But the neglect of supposedly secondary things—the problems of race, cities, education, and the environment—led us unerringly to the distemper and distorted priorities of the 1950's and 1960's.

Our world outlook in 1945 was remarkably mature: we had a nuclear monopoly, but did not brandish a Big Stick; there were a few flourishes of vainglory and little of the victor's arrogance. The note of triumph was sober and thoughtful. This was a fine moment in American history. Some of the best aspects of our national character were on display. The catholicity of Jefferson, the magnanimity of Lincoln, the shrewd sense of enlightened self-interest of Theodore Roosevelt, the idealism of Woodrow Wilson and Franklin D. Roosevelt were all visible to the world in 1945 and the early postwar years. These and a sense of mission stemming from the one-world concept enabled our international statesmanship to express the full measure of the promise of American democracy.

By contrast, our thoughts about the problems we faced at home were piecemeal, shortsighted, and highly personal. Most of us had a spacious and color-blind concept of the family of nations we hoped to nurture, but no intention of admitting the Negro to full citizenship in our own family. We had no clear idea of the postwar society we wanted to build. (Hindsight tells us that one of the vital missed op-

11

portunities of the war was President Roosevelt's failure to permit the organization of voluntary integrated fighting units—a step that would have expedited postwar action on what was then called "the Negro problem.")

On the overriding issues, the 1946 consensus was correct: there would be no hope for world order unless the United States maintained the power and diplomacy to keep the peace; but at the same time our power and purpose would falter unless the economic system functioned well enough to sustain our strength and self-confidence. The global view and vision were unimpaired. But within our courtyard, a myopia occurred, and we began to reap the results of unbalanced policies and politics. As citizens of the world, we had learned the hard lessons of Woodrow Wilson; and we were ready to try out F.D.R.'s notion that our economy could be made to function to full capacity in peacetime. But when it came to new national goals and new efforts to remake the environment, we were half haunted by the Great Depression and half ready for something akin to the postwar "normalcy" of Harding. Our ideas of growth were self-centered, disparate, and self-contradictory; personal, not social. We were individually ready to settle for a job, a house, good food, a share of consumer goods, and a little leisure as acceptable home-front attainments.

There were two things wrong with this outlook. First, it laid its main emphasis on personal satisfactions and ignored higher and broader aspirations. Second, its almost exclusive preference for these private satisfactions over public needs (as John Kenneth Galbraith would make plain in 1958 in *The Affluent Society*) ensured that the over-all environment would be shabby, soiled, and second-rate. Our aim was for autos, not a balanced transportation system; for houses, not close-knit communities; for school buildings, not superior instruction. We were consciously, and on a piecemeal basis, choosing the material things denied us in the 1930's and the war years, rather than the larger interrelated systems and goals the new technologies could have made possible in the 1950's. This was an open invitation to the old individualistic approach to "progress" recorded only by indices of quantity, and was hostile to any proposals for spacious public projects that could have elevated American life.

All this was apparent in the uninspired leadership that came from politicians and planners. When the war ended, no architects or planners stepped forward, or were asked to, with bold plans to renew the core cities and build graceful new towns in the suburbs. There was a vast indifference to the slow rot of the old cities. The plans and prophecies of Lewis Mumford were ignored. No Daniel Burnham appeared to urge that we eschew "little plans." No American "Bauhaus" came along to revolutionize our ideas of building. Quite the contrary: everywhere little plans were the order of the day.

On the issue of equality, it was a Swede, Gunnar Myrdal, not a native scholar or statesman, who, in 1944, near the end of the war, warned in *An American Dilemma* that the American dream would become a nightmare if the Negro was denied full fellowship and full opportunity in our democracy.

And the quiescence and narrow perspective of the postwar conservation movement did little to redirect the urbanization and industrial growth that would befoul the air, turn rivers into open sewers, and overrun the countryside with "slurbs" and scars and eyesores. The bulldozer, the billboard, and the belching smokestack were the authentic emblems of postwar progress.

Again the backward look, the pull of past history, and

13

the desire to demobilize and build no more than our private lives betrayed us. Many urgent and legitimate ambitions were circumscribed by the beliefs and easy generalizations of another generation: the unexamined assumption that the unmelted minorities would be content to remain servile, second-class citizens at the edges of our national life; the unexamined assumption that slums were an inevitable part of urban America; the unexamined assumption that the problems of the urban areas were "local" phenomena unworthy of national concern, and the unexamined assumption that any industrialized nation had to be a filthy, unclean country. This series of uncritically accepted assumptions was braided into a chain of myths and priorities, which formed the basis for the overpowering postwar paradox of American life: our readiness to attempt revolutionary advance in the world at large and our domestic willingness to settle for materialistic mediocrity.

If world order required enormous investments to stimulate and sustain the economic growth of friendly countries, we would respond with a dynamic Marshall Plan, with generous foreign aid, and, by the early 1960's, with a challenging Alliance for Progress for the Americas and a humanitarian Peace Corps for the world. If world peace meant strong-nerved diplomacy, the round-the-clock maintenance of a nuclear deterrent, and a vast and costly defense establishment, we would be ready to parry the Communist thrust with force and diplomacy, as in Berlin, Korea, and Cuba. We were ready to make whatever input of public and private brain power and budgets were necessary to preserve our scientific supremacy. Technology's triumphs were so swift and varied that we had the atomic age, the jet age, the space age, and the age of automation in the short space of fifteen years. Technical "know-how" was now the supreme expression of our national prowess, and each success of applied science gave the managers of the military-industrial system first call on budgets and scientific talent. Our efforts to build missile systems, put men in outer space, and construct supersonic aircraft confirmed our wartime faith that "crash" efforts and Manhattan-style projects would make "the impossible" possible. The credo was "Can do!"

These feats of technology confused our purpose and produced a massive diversion of energy and resources toward the overachievement of military and industrial goals and away from what might have been the more creative pursuits of civilized society. These technical tours de force became a specious national exercise in mountain climbing (embodied, above all, in the overglamorized manned space program), which gave us a sense of adventure without commitment. We were thus disarmed for the tougher task of achieving those social goals and community objectives that can never be attained without the deep personal involvement of a majority of our citizens. This fact the Kerner Commission rediscovered as the central cause of the violence in the summer of 1967.

The very pace of technical progress served to sharpen the paradox. We produced, for example, more autos, trucks, and civilian aircraft than all other nations combined, and our engineers and builders engaged in the largest road, residential, industrial, and commercial construction programs in world history. Only in rocket propulsion did we yield leadership to another nation—and even here national pride demanded, and got, a crash effort to catch up.

But speed without sufficient thought about where we were going was too much a part of the national pattern. We began annually to kill nearly fifty thousand people in

15

auto accidents, yearly to maim nearly two million as a result of a preference for road speed over highway safety, for horsepower over sound engineering. Mislocated airports made the lives of millions miserable, and freeways needlessly sliced up cities, making noise, congestion, and foul air an inescapable part of the urban milieu. Our auto obsession made road-building the main handmaiden of "development," and multiple auto ownership the badge of personal success. A roads-for-cars-only approach to transportation drove the cyclist, walker, and horseman from the scene. Our preoccupation with speed so impaired our ability to see that the late Frank Dobie was heard to lament, "We Americans don't travel any more, we're just transported."

The seventy per cent of our people who lived on one per cent of the land urgently needed convenient mass-transit systems. Detroit's engineers and the aerospace technicians could have designed them. The United States, however, did not put into operation a single modern mass-transit plan from 1945 to 1968. Japan built "bullet trains" to connect its largest cities. Montreal's subway system made New York's look like a rattletrap in a medieval dungeon. But we were determined to stick with our auto-freeway formula even if it strangled our cities and shortened our lives.

Our option in favor of suburban sprawl constituted a conscious avoidance of a clear preference for wise growth. A penchant for planless, individualistic "development" shortchanged the homeowner. Like the land raiders of the nineteenth century who leveled the forests and slaughtered the buffalo, the speculator-developers who now carved up the countryside were looked on as the honored agents of necessary growth. Build-and-run land speculation led inevitably to nontown Levittowns. We wanted housing, not humane communities. And that is what we got—with the developers acting as the chosen instruments of an inchoate policy of urban expansion. Their formula was quite simple: buy an attractive outlying tract, treat it as commodity, cut it up into same-size lots, bulldoze them into salable shapes, get a federally guaranteed mortgage, build structures, advertise them as "estates," throw in a shopping center, call it a community—and let the county worry about schools, amenities, and the general environment—and move on to the next development.

In building, the new technology never had a chance; we had a paucity of planners who unveiled dreams of communities for tomorrow. The building trades, their segregated unions, and the builders stuck to post-and-beam construction, too tied to old ways to let innovation get a foot in the door. In the large cities, we constructed at random presumably efficient boxes geared to front-footage economics that too often ignored the human scale. We could readily have developed the technical skills to build handsome cities, but our commitment to catch-as-catch-can speculation precluded the attempt.

We would not plan. We did not love the land. The result was termed by a visiting British planner in the mid-1950's the "mess that is man-made America." The phrase fit, and it has stuck. We chose not to "do the impossible" in the arena where we acted out our daily lives.

Whether it builds an Appian Way, an Acropolis, a Great Wall, a Petrograd, a Lyceum, or a Chartres Cathedral, a nation's public works and undertakings mirror the state of mind of its ruling class, or, in a democracy, reveal something about the inner convictions of its people. We embarked on three domestic projects in the postwar period that, taken together, reveal much about the turn of mind of the time. Each involved the planned investment of

17

many billions over a fixed period of years; each had a clear-cut goal; each involved the whole nation; each was an expression of a priority and a purpose.

The G.I. Bill of Rights, enacted just before the end of World War II, was the first of these projects. As part of a program of veterans' benefits, it proved to be an inspired investment in education. When the Korean War eligibles were added, it cost about twenty-one billion dollars. Yet it must rank as one of our most productive social programs of the postwar period. Because of it, there was no "lost generation" of World War II, and it gave fresh impetus to our educational and cultural institutions. The other two projects—the interstate highway program of 1956 and the space program of 1961—expressed our preference for vast engineering projects. Both entailed huge investments in machines, both enhanced the mobility of man, and both have had the overwhelming support of the American people, although neither is directly designed to improve the quality of life in this country or assist in urban renovation or racial reconciliation. The country needed to build highways and wanted to explore space, to be sure, but why were these the only huge national projects to gain an exclusive call on the public purse? President John F. Kennedy gave a clue to the answer when he noted ruefully in 1961 that the Congress was not ready to make dramatic decisions to upgrade education, rejuvenate the cities, or integrate the Negro even were he to propose that the man-in-space money be spent for such purposes.

Analysis shows that a combination of two forces caused us to key our expectations at a median level. First, there was the imperious and insatiable claim of defense on the national exchequer and the readiness of Congressmen to err always on the side of overpreparedness and overkill when it came to national security. Second, there were the

18

inherent weaknesses of our political institutions, which were magnified by two crucial cleavages: the old North-South division on race (which the Kerner Commission has now diagnosed as a nationwide infection of racism), and the rural-urban tug of war on national priorities. These combined to limit the effectiveness of our politics, and deprived us of the unity we needed to make the larger, harder choices.

Nuclear weapons and the issue of survival forced consensus in foreign affairs, and the Congress enjoyed a fine hour on the world scene. But beyond a generalized agreement on the goals of full production and full employment, expressed in the Employment Act of 1946, which enunciated a national policy and established a Council of Economic Advisers to the President, it was apparent that our national legislature was unable to make bold decisions to reshape our ambitions and institutions. The cleavages were too deep, too fundamental, to permit a broader consensus. Consequently, the Washington dialogue became an arid debate over the completion of the New Deal.

Our dynamic new technology made the depression-preventing panaceas of the 1930's outdated. But the Congress gave scant attention as it argued about erecting housing instead of building new communities, and tinkered with the Social Security Act, the minimum wage, and price supports for farmers. Unable to come to grips with the big issues, the Congress for two decades was embroiled in divisive debates about federal aid to education, civil rights, health care for the elderly, and assistance for urban areas. Why did Washington discuss "housing" when the British Parliament was erecting "new towns"? Why did Great Britain provide immediate medical care for the elderly, while we blathered about it for years?

One answer is that the overwhelming postwar mandate

given to the Labour government made sweeping social reforms politically practicable. The House of Commons was a much more flexible instrument of the national will than our hidebound legislative institutions. The Senate filibuster, the seniority system, the malapportionment of the House (and the state legislatures), the disfranchisement of the Southern Negro, all perpetuated rural control and lodged effective power in a coalition of minorities more concerned with the annual balancing of budgets than with promoting the general welfare. Congress in the postwar years was basically a turn-of-the-century institution; it was anti-Negro, anticity, antieducation, anticulture, and incapable of thinking in terms of national goals for an over-all environment of quality, human equality, and ecological balance. Those who favored the racial *status quo* were in substantial control of the political process. While a predominantly dark-skinned world looked on, the Congress was unable to pass simple statutes to curb lynching, to abolish the poll tax, to assure the simple right to vote, or to enact general aid for the education of all children.

Rural control could be measured in a number of ways. In the first postwar budgets the federal government appropriated more money for research on plant and animal diseases than on the diseases of humans. More federal dollars were spent on instructing farmers how to farm than on elementary and secondary education. As late as 1965, much more money was appropriated for direct aid to agriculture than for aid to the urban areas where seventy per cent of the people lived in an atmosphere of heightening crisis.

The federal government was an active accomplice in the defiling of the environment. The Federal Housing Administration was the midwife of suburban sprawl. Government installations, not just private industry, polluted air and water. The deliberate indiscipline of federal aid for highways actually encouraged the erection of hideous billboard alleys. Federal leadership was so purblind that as late as 1955 a Secretary of the Interior asserted that he saw no need to expand the national park system, and a prairie-bred President in 1960 vetoed a weak water-pollution-control bill on the ground that it usurped local prerogatives.

It was increasingly clear by the mid-1950's that built-in rural domination and deep differences on race had produced a partial paralysis of politics. Inaction had induced decay and discontent. Negro anger was rising, the cancerous tentacles of pollution were reaching everywhere, the underfinanced cities were floundering, megalopolis was reaching ever outward, and an unnoticed migration of millions of Negroes and other disadvantaged poor into urban centers was under way. The obvious solutions, however, were foreclosed by antiquated politics.

In one of the sublime ironies of U.S. history, the Supreme Court became the catalyst that induced a resolution of the dilemma. The Court—not the executive or the legislative branch of government—made the most momentous decisions of the postwar period and thus profoundly altered the possibilities of American life. This activist impulse of the Court was tinctured with incongruity, for in the aftermath of the Civil War it did more to nullify the Emancipation Proclamation and undo the liberating work of Lincoln than any other national institution. Now, when the people and their elected spokesmen were immobilized, the same insulated Court of nine men became the saving agent of change. The opinions in *Brown* v. *Board of Education* and the "one-man one-vote" case were acts of atonement. These decisions were a long overdue updating of the Constitution to conform to twentieth-century views of

21

human rights. With great solemnity the Court declared the idea of apartness incompatible with the idea of equality; it took Jefferson at his word and at last stripped the quotation marks from the majestic phrase "all men are created equal." In 1954 the Brown case was a moral imperative for this country; in 1962 the one-man one-vote decision was a political imperative for a balanced American growth.

A large segment of the Congress fought the Court, and the gentle man who was President when the 1954 decision was handed down was unable to understand the drastic modifications of our national life implicit in its mandate. A hundred years of history were compressed into a few short years by the Court's audacious reinterpretation of the Constitution. It radically altered the expectations of all "second-class" citizens—and also set the stage for the turbulence of the 1960's.

The Kennedy-Johnson years saw a largely successful effort to settle the long dispute over social legislation and quicken the pace of social change. Defense expenditures started to level off, and the success of the "new economics" brought a steady expansion of the gross national product and the promise of bigger budgets to finance long-deferred public-sector projects at home. When the climactic Eighty-ninth Congress enacted the first effective civil-rights legislation, the first general federal aid to education, and a medical-care plan for the aged, hopes rose that the Great Society blueprint of President Lyndon B. Johnson would take hold as well as had F.D.R.'s New Deal.

However, a crucial crossroad decision in early 1965 produced a new and major shift of emphasis. At the very moment that a turbulent human-rights crisis was ready to erupt in the ghettos of our largest cities, a decision was made to place a huge expeditionary force in the jungles of

22

Southeast Asia. It would consume federal funds needed for vital problem-solving projects at home. This tragic coincidence dominated—and frustrated—the political life of the nation in 1968. It deepened the disaffection of the blacks, the poor, and the college students. It cast legitimate doubt upon the wisdom of spending billions of dollars to put a man on the moon while shaken cities writhed with unrest. It forced President Johnson to put aside all personal ambition and seek a negotiated peace in Vietnam. Tortured by this coincidence, and brutalized by the horror of the assassinations of Dr. Martin Luther King, Jr., and Senator Robert F. Kennedy, the American Dream slid into momentary nightmare.

2. The Urban Affliction

"... There is not the slightest doubt any longer that we are losing our very special, God-given chance to create in this country a form, an order, a high civilization. This simply cannot be done in a physical setting of crashing vulgarity in the cities and dreary uniformity in the suburbs." —ERIC SEVAREID

Since 1965 the American political and social systems have been confronted by a test more demanding and ominous than any in the country's domestic history except the Civil War. This crisis represents the confluence of two tragic tributaries of failure: the century-long failure to build livable cities and the closely related failure to make a multiracial society work.

The trials of the nation in facing these failures have been painfully visible in fire, in violence, in the anguish of organized protest, in the anger and chaos of civil disorder, and in the extreme alienation of youth. U.S. citizens have openly advocated the wrecking of our cities, college cam-

24

puses have seethed with protest, and a sense of community has disappeared in some urban sectors. For the first time since General Sherman's scorched-earth march to the sea in 1865, our cities have been put to the torch by Americans. These tragic occurrences and attitudes threaten the vitals of our system. They cast doubt on our ability to make the dream of brotherhood a reality. They call into question the competence of industry and government to eliminate poverty. They throw a garish spotlight on the failure of American urbanization. And they question both the quality of our leadership and the adaptability of our institutions.

No sudden lapse led to this emergency. In large measure it is the outgrowth of old errors and of shortcomings of previous generations. The seeds were planted by public and private policies of keeping a whole race in an inferior state; by approaches to economics that accepted poverty and slums as inevitable incidents of American life; by a division of power that strangled local government and demeaned local leadership; by a national default of conscience which produced the degradation of the environment; by the belief that producing goods for man was more important than the cultivation of the good in man. The truth is that our cities were on fire decades before the first flames at Watts. But the conflagration was, to use a phrase of Robert Frost's, "the slow, smokeless burning of decay." Yet, when physicians were finally put on the case (and the Cassandra-like forecasts of Lewis Mumford read plain) , the diagnoses were consistent and clear-cut.

After the summer riots of 1967, at a time when the nation could boast of the most prolonged peacetime prosperity in history, a Detroit businessman peered into the pus-pocket slums of his city and exclaimed: "Absolutely terrifying. No wonder people riot." And Arnold Toynbee, always quick with prophecy, observed, "America seems to be heading for . . . a kind of permanent civil war within the principal cities of the United States." This was considered an alarmist judgment by most Americans. Conventional wisdom had held for two decades that a physical reconditioning of the slums would somehow arrest the destructive effects of race discrimination, and enough jobs would turn up to make life gradually better for the more than six million migrants who poured, unprepared, into the decaying cities of the North. The velocity of this mass migration can be indicated by two statistics: between 1960 and 1967 New Haven's nonwhite population rose from fifteen to twenty-four per cent; Newark's rose from thirty-four to fifty-two per cent.

Slums, however, were only the worst sores on a sick urban body. Architect Edward Durell Stone looked at the U.S. cityscape and scathingly described it as "a main street with its neon wilderness, architecture without beauty or distinction, streets snarled up in automobiles, no harmony, no beauty, few trees, limited park areas . . . nothing but an asphalt jungle where the big idea is to sell merchandise, put gas in the automobile, and move on." Stone was right, but, given the blighted urban scene, right in a way that ironically subverts the best values of his own fine work. The cruelest part of the irony lies in society's limited use of men like Stone. To confine architecture, as Americans almost always do, to single structures rather than over-all designs is to guarantee that what few good buildings are built will be imbedded in personal or corporate privacy and make virtually no contribution to the essential fabric of the city.

Other self-appointed physicians of sick cities have echoed Stone's judgment: an eminent architect wondered aloud whether American cities were "too ugly to save"; a sensitive editor termed our largest city, New York, "something of an insult"; a *Fortune* writer, back from a nationwide tour, asserted that "the United States has let its public environment run to overpowering disorder," and concluded that "the whole place needs to be done over," and an elderly architect chided his countrymen for turning one of the "most beautiful continents into one of the ugliest" in the short space of half a century.

This spate of criticism raises basic questions. Why do we linger outside the door of distinction, so rich and so slovenly, so friendly and so filled with hate? Why should a people prideful of its science settle for a soiled and second-rate environment? Why has the most science-centered society in history *not* developed a science of human settlements? Why is our industrial complex able to build Saturn rockets but unable to fashion tools to renovate and renew the environment where most of us live? Why, if it is sound to spend billions of dollars on supersonic aircraft to whisk us to London in two hours, is it not equally important to devise systems of public transportation to get most of us to and from work in less than half that time? Above all, why have we been so slow to come to grips with the domestic shortcomings that vitiate the best intentions of our foreign policies?

The answers to some of these questions lie, of course, in our history. Until now we have possessed this continent and prepared our living spaces on it more with rapacity than with regard for man, more with force of machine power than with vision. In attempting to reconstruct the flaws that led to failure, one encounters a vicious circle of attitudes and events that have shaped our large and small municipalities. Agrarian roots and the rural suspicion of two centuries taught us to distrust city conglomerations; distrust led to the rigging of arrangements (rotten boroughs and rural malapportionment were only the most notorious disfranchising devices), which seriously weakened city action; weak city government led to a system of low priorities, then to even lower citizen expectations of the capability of local government. Low expectations, in turn, led to weak leadership; weak leadership led to lack of control over growth, and onward to the waste of the resources and opportunities of cities. Finally, waste and improvidence led to supposedly "insoluble" problems, and insoluble problems meant that cities were indeed "ungovernable." Thus the ring closed back to the anticity bias where it all began.

Another circle of failure and frustration revolved around the racial issue. A legalized policy of apartness, sanctioned by broadly based private opinion, for nearly a century shaped a two-color caste system in American society. This caste system was accepted by city builders, catering to the market, who began to create vast homogeneous areas within and around the cities. People preferred to live together with their look-alike, be-alike brethren and would willingly commute many miles in order to place a safe distance between their private lives and the everyday world of business. This American way resulted in a large-scale pattern of urban sprawl and suburban segregation. It was quite possible in the suburban sameness for a child to play, go to school, and grow up without really knowing human beings of other races or classes. This was socially suffocating and further entrenched the mistrust of the egalitarian brotherhood propounded by Jefferson and reaffirmed by Lincoln. Thus another ring was closed, and became a formidable fortress against the influx of rural Negroes as they moved toward their new "homes" in the central cities. The truth of the matter was that, without quite knowing it, we were trying a unique and potentially ennobling experiment for the first time in the history of civilization—the establishment of a multiracial society—but our private commitment fell far short of our professed principles.

The historical development of our cities was determined by piecemeal decisions that bespoke the urgencies of commerce, geography, and prejudice, not the needs of a mature civilization. Initially, they grew beside the natural harbors of the seacoast and along rivers, where water-borne shipments of goods and people were convenient. Many of them sprang up overnight; others straggled into existence in shapes created by the short-view vectors of free enterprise. It has been pointed out by Charles Abrams that in the empire-building era that followed the Civil War the horse did more to shape most cities than the early architects. As Abrams puts it: "The distance he could draw a tram to work places, and the distance and speed a team of horses could pull a fire engine, determined the boundaries of a neighborhood. It was an era of equine city planning, equine streets, equine architecture, and equine industrialization. The age was equine even in its effect on personality, for it slowed human pace to that of the horse whose limitations conditioned man's ideals."

The life of the urban dweller and his values were consistently submerged and sacrificed. Railroads were rammed into the heart of most cities; the asphalt and steel bands of highways and railroads took the water fronts and riversides from the people; and, as the twentieth century progressed, land speculation and the automobile largely determined the face and character of the cities.

At the same time, there was a certain beauty to life in the small towns, enhanced by the physical proximity of all sorts and conditions of men. Though the rich man lived on the corner and the Negro, even here discriminated against, lived in "the back" or over the stable or garage, they were

29

in contact; their lives were at least tangentially related. But this, too, was lost as the cities grew in size beyond all rational bounds.

European-style city-making was alien to our experience. The architect side of Jefferson's nature "envied Europe their art," but even he never expected much of our cities. It was not that we disdained design, but, rather, that we had designed a political system that denied cities the power or wherewithal to create greatness, and made improvised development become the American way. The planning and building of great cities, as Solon and Phidias found in ancient Athens, is always a task for teamwork. Detail is important, control even more so, and the undertaking must enlist the talents and co-operation of the entire community. But our genius has run to parts, not wholes. We have been builders of efficient, soaring buildings, not master builders of city complexes. Our one notable contribution to architecture is the skyscraper—a singular structural stunt that somehow symbolized both the excess of individualism that has brought us to the edge of urban bankruptcy and the readiness to employ steel without style and put technology before taste.

Great cities put people first. They use land lovingly to create the kind of large and small boulevards, plazas, malls, vistas, squares, and waterscapes which form the *ambiance* of London, Paris, Rotterdam, Florence, and Athens. In our country, only in the nation's capital does space and distance dominate and define a significant part of the setting. The squares and circles and spaces of Washington show what control and planning can do to make a city unique. Only Washington limits the height of all buildings by law. Its vistas allow its monuments to soar; its low buildings soften the handiwork of man and give trees a chance to spread the good tidings of a green sheath. Only in Washington, of all our major cities, do the spires of cathedrals still dominate the horizon and deny the message of the skyscraper sky line that we are pre-eminently and everlastingly a commercial civilization. But even the nation's capital is only a partial triumph, for beyond its spires and spaces lie the ugly enclaves of ghettos.

Our Phidiases—Frederick Law Olmsted and Daniel Burnham—had only a brief hour at the edge of things; and Frank Lloyd Wright, the most renowned American designer of this century, never completed a structure built with public funds in his seventy years as an architect. The most esteemed Americans of the last century were not apostles of urban design. They were, instead, inventors, single-minded captains of industry, and imaginative engineers. It did not occur to the Carnegies, Edisons, Rockefellers, Roeblings, and Fords of an earlier era to turn their talents away from machines and industrial efficiency to the creation of superior cities. Machine production and great feats of engineering, not the manufacture of elegant, highly livable cities, were the objective.

The last three generations of Americans have exploited the cities as surely as our nineteenth-century ancestors stripped and raided the forestlands of this continent. For every corporation or individual who gave an asset to the people, a hundred selfishly subtracted from the common wealth. Every unwise rezoning for ill-planned buildings robbed us of sky, a sense of space, a glimpse of greenery. Poor transportation systems robbed men of time, and a rising crescendo of noise robbed them of peace and privacy. Worst of all, laws that discouraged the uprooting of slums gave birth to superghettos and robbed everyone of the precious fellowship of neighborhood feeling.

But one must quickly acknowledge that this robbery was as legal as the leveling of the forests, for more often than

31

not local officials paved the way for the developers who gradually dehumanized the cities. "Take," not "give"; "hasten," not "consider"—these were the cardinal rules. And when, in New York, farsighted men built Rockefeller Center—a plaza with a fountain and open space enclosed by office skyscrapers—the shock was so great that it took nearly a generation for imitators to step forward and repeat this spacious gesture.

It is a sad fact that governments often conspired to encourage the forces of disorder and decay. The federal government abetted fragmentation and encouraged non-planning. The Federal Housing Administration actively encouraged the worst forms of suburban sprawl. Federal public-housing programs more often than not replaced the old slums with superslums of tomorrow, and all too often urban renewal was perverted into Negro removal. Until the late 1960's federal aid for air and water-pollution control was negligible. The one vast public-works program of the 1950's—the highway act of 1956—sliced up cities and compounded the congestion of car-inundated streets.

The squandering of the land, water, air, light, sky, and open space of our cities has been the conservation scandal of this century. The misuse of our water estate is a case in point. No nation has ever had more superb, water-based sites for cities; the settings of San Francisco, New York, Seattle, San Diego, Chicago, Boston, and St. Louis, to name but a few, were unsurpassed. With wise land-use planning, their rivers and lakes and harbors might have been the threads on which could be strung beads of beauty and order. Yet most of our cities have fouled and marred and depleted these assets. New York has more water front than any city in the world—five hundred and forty miles of it, with thirty-five miles of beaches—but untreated sewage, misplaced highways, and rotting clutter have cut off New

32

Yorkers from their own shorelands. San Francisco's incomparable bay, insulted in every way known to mechanized man, is now misshapen and reduced in beauty and humane value. Many of the water-oriented cities of the Great Lakes area and the Mississippi basin paradoxically are forced to look landward for outdoor recreation and lakeward for new airport sites. By contrast, Italy's Venice, the only city to make optimum use of a water endowment, is, many agree, one of the most serene and enjoyable urban areas in all the world, albeit a static relic of a frozen past.

The dissipation of irreplaceable land has been equally appalling. Today, most cities waste most of their streets, as well as most of their open space, their water fronts, their vistas, their riverscapes, their parks. Fifty acres for cars and streets and parking lots and one, if any, for playgrounds is the apparent policy of most cities.

If, as President John F. Kennedy once noted, the wise use of resources is "the highest form of national thrift," we have indeed been profligate. Nowhere is this more so than in California, an area with the finest over-all climate of North America. There, glistening air, majestic mountainscapes, unspoiled beaches, and a lovely landscape of orchards and farms and small cities have been swallowed up in an orgy of land speculation, untrammeled commercialism, and bulldozed progress. Nor is there tangible hope for salvation by technology in many parts of Southern California. The large-lot sprawl of five decades has so thinly and evenly spread the population across the valleys that mass transit is now unfeasible and a proliferation of high-speed freeways is the only form of "relief" so far found possible. In this automobile-centered environment, U.C.L.A. now charges its students more for parking space than for tuition.

In this area of California can be found all the accumulated ills of unplanned growth: exclusive reliance on the most inefficient means of transportation (the individual auto) ; an enormous waste of time in travel; the triumph of the shopping center and the decline of the neighborhood; the garish crescendo of the commercial strip-highway and the Chinese-wall invasions of the omnipresent freeway; the expenditure of billions of dollars for highways (so people can "escape" to the beaches) but only pennies for parklands so desperately needed in every neighborhood; an apparent consensus that the highest and best use of urban land—and even the air itself—is for automotive, not human, activity. This is, in fact, the final triumph of machines over men. The small-grained scale that once invited a safe stroll, a hike, or a bicycle outing and the multipurpose, but always human, use of streets have been lost. Is it any wonder that Watts, a rotting cul-de-sac in the heart of the nation's least controlled explosion of suburban sprawl, was the first urban ghetto to blow up and burn?

As long as local governments lacked budgets, plans, and power, and were dedicated to the proposition that any growth was acceptable, no new or exciting approaches to metropolitan progress were possible. We were a pragmatic, individualistic people, and if new industrial activity promised payrolls, no other questions were asked. Industry was welcome, and if the entrepreneurs gouged a community and mortgaged its future by building a hideous plant that usurped open space and emitted effluents that ruined a river or befouled the air, this was acceptable, whether it was a pulp mill in an unspoiled valley in Idaho or North Carolina, a packing house in Omaha, or a steel mill on the Great Lakes. Urban environments have become the end products of misguided concepts of property

34

rights and short-term profits. This is a conclusion we never grasped.

The warping of the few good land-use plans that we did have also played a part in the rape of metropolitan values. To this day, breaking zoning regulations is a game played with zest, and considerable success, in most cities. A single vignette of suburban development dramatizes the sorry story and reveals a fatal weakness of local government as well. The rezoning of Merrywood, on the palisades of the Potomac near Washington, occurred in 1963. Among the participants were a county sheriff who acted as "broker," a group of developers, a suave zoning lawyer, and a Board of Supervisors (some of whose members were later convicted of conspiracy for actions in other rezoning cases). Rezoning was granted to allow high-rise apartments on the Potomac Palisades. This violated the metropolitan master plan, and in the end it was thwarted only by the purchase of a scenic easement by the National Park Service at a cost of nearly a million dollars.

Local government has not worked well in this country because we have not given it a fighting chance to function; its entities have been too weak to plan, too poor to act. But this, after all, was intended when we made the cities the starved stepchildren of government. Glib talk about "ungovernable" cities is a rationalization that masks an unwillingness to revitalize local governments and permit large-scale urban renovation to begin. Weak city and county government is the foreseeable result of past practices. Rural-run legislatures and Congresses have rationed local power and retained the superior sources of revenue. The "lower" governments have been saddled with welfare and public-education costs that in most modern countries are paid for by central governments. At the same time, the "higher" bureaucracies have sat by complacently while the overpowering problems of poverty, pollution, and racial discord were piled on the doorsteps of underfinanced, undermanned, and already floundering urban governments.

With such handicaps and disabilities, the lag of leadership at city hall is easy to understand. Politics, like physics, has its own immutable laws. One is: weak politics repels excellence and attracts mediocrity. The nineteenth century put the outrageous Boss Tweed in the history books, but beyond Tom L. Johnson, of Cleveland, who took office in 1901, who are the mayors the nation remembers in the twentieth century? Who have been the inspirers and innovators? How many truly great mayors have reinvigorated urban institutions and presided over the refurbishing of their cities? The names are pitifully few; that much is certain. Of course, flamboyant mayors like "Big Bill" Thompson, of Chicago, Michael Curley, of Boston, and New York's Jimmy Walker found a place in memory as shrewd showmen who entertained the populace while they presided over the slow decay of their cities. Tied to the patronage politics which captured the votes of the minority groups in the melting pot, unaware of the basic elements of urban grace, they readily sacrificed future livability to the selfish ambitions of developers and the agents of industrial growth. For all his panache, what, one is tempted to inquire, is the municipal legacy Fiorello La Guardia left New York? How well did he prepare his city for the postwar onslaught of change? For all his temporary triumphs in moving traffic, will not Robert Moses be remembered more for the wetlands and beaches he saved than for all his asphalt and bridges? And is it not sadly significant that New York City's most vivid postwar figure until John Lindsay took office in 1966 was the official "greeter," Grover Whalen, rather than any leader who attempted to modernize and humanize our most "vibrant" city?

Across the nation, leadership failed to involve the talents of industry and the design sector in the effort for municipal betterment. Until the riots of the 1960's, few businessmen bothered to involve themselves and their organizations in the future of the city. They paid their taxes, complained, commuted to the far edge of megalopolis—and left the rest to city hall. As for leadership from the design professions, the paucity of gifted city planners in this century is noteworthy. Apart from Daniel Burnham, of Chicago, and the younger Olmsted (and even they dealt too much in superficialities), one must race ahead to the last decade, to the work of Edward Logue in Boston and Edmund Bacon in Philadelphia, to find bold concepts and broad vision. Architects, it seemed, could be counted on to design individual buildings, but were not enlisted for the larger task of saving the city. After making a thankful bow to the best mayors of recent times—Richard Lee, of New Haven, David Lawrence, of Pittsburgh, Joseph Clark, of Philadelphia, Raymond Tucker, of St. Louis, and maybe William Hartsfield, John Collins, Jerome Cavanagh, and John Lindsay—one realizes how few of these excellent men have been able to marshal the energy, insight, and power needed to carry out large-scale projects to reshape entire cities.

It is, therefore, understandable that the best examples of city planning in this country grew out of tightly controlled and carefully implemented master plans. For example, both Washington, D.C., and Salt Lake City were offshoots not of ordinary politics but of authoritarian circumstance. L'Enfant could plan because he was the agent of a Founding Father who was authorized to plan a capital; Brigham

Young could lay out Salt Lake City because he was the unquestioned leader of a theocratic state. But these efforts were atypical and ran against the American grain. Catch-as-catch-can speculative building, small-time profiteers, and racial bigotry were to fix the frame and face of most municipalities.

Unfortunately, even those social surgeons who correctly diagnosed the big-city sickness found their remedies impeded by the vested interests and obsolete institutions. Sound cities were impossible if outmoded charters forbade regional solutions to the over-all problems. How could there be a common plan or good design or programs of environmental rehabilitation when no one could do anything about upriver pollution, upwind air contamination, or the care and keeping of the land itself?

The whole sad story is epitomized by the political plight of metropolitan New York, with its seventeen county governments and five hundred autonomous zoning boards. How can the hopes and needs of such disparate groups be welded into a whole and wholesome entity? Westchester county, a classic piece of the metropolitan mosaic, itself has twenty-eight independent "master plans," thirty-seven different subdivision regulations, thirty-eight "official" maps, forty-four zoning regulations, two hundred and fifteen members of assorted planning groups, two hundred and eighty members of legislative boards, two hundred and forty-five school trustees, and twenty-eight members of county commissions.

With no agreement on common principles of planning, such diverse and numerous voices can only shout in the discord of competing ideas and conflicting standards that will inevitably doom entire regions to no-plan plans, to citizen apathy, and to localized aims and commonplace aspirations. If growth is to be decided *ad hoc,* by the day-to-

day whims and maneuverings of "just grow" land speculation, random development will decide the shape and scale
of the American city and guarantee a man-made mess of
continental proportions. This, of course, has been a reflection of the inner drive of the suburbanite to establish
easygoing environments insulated, temporarily at least,
from the problems of interracial fellowship and high property taxes.

Into this complacent system, between 1950 and 1968, six
million Southern Negroes spilled northward, bearing with
them all the accumulated disabilities of a demoralizing
social system that had left them wholly unprepared to
succeed in the cities. The only reception these "immigrants" got was joblessness and the cold hospitality of a
demeaning system of social welfare. This new American
melting pot quickly became a cold cauldron of frustrated
hopes. Unsolved human problems multiplied in urban
areas functionally incapable of dealing with them. So we
came, with slow understanding, to what we now call the
"urban crisis of the 1960's."

Now that history has unmistakably certified our failures,
I am convinced that it is a stroke of fortune that the many
overriding issues of cities and human relations interlock
and overlap. We cannot solve one problem without resolving the total problem; we must, as part of a single, unprecedented project, build beautiful cities and attempt to
become a beautiful people ourselves. To reheat our melting pot, and stir it wisely and well, will require that the
issues of racial fellowship, slums, ghettos, and urban imbalance be dealt with together, as part of an inspiring
national plan. The miscalled "Negro problem" is now
subsumed under the larger issue of how to redefine good
cities and the good life in this country.

No great city will ever just grow. It must express a

vision, a plan. There can be no common glory in a free society without a common plan, and such a plan can only exist as an expression of public purpose. The many mansions of the radiant city involve far more than the furnishing of attractive rooms for individual living. This is the lesson we have yet to learn.

There are some hopeful signs. Some leaders of business, labor, politics, and design are beginning to understand that the cities cannot be saved without their aid. But it is time to acknowledge that our troubles are too acute for repair work, little plans, or the patchwork programs of "urban renewal." Indeed, one can hope the turning point was reached sometime in the 1960's. In the last month of his life, in a noble address at Amherst, President John F. Kennedy elevated his gaze to "Look forward to the day when we will build handsome and balanced cities . . . ," and a few months later his successor, Lyndon B. Johnson, made city renewal a central theme of his Great Society program.

But the hard realities of the 1960's—the squalor, the ugliness, the inhumanity, and the police squads at the ready—tell us that the failure of American urbanization is now a judgment of history. The urban malady is severe and pervasive. Experience has taught us the hard lesson that far more is required than palliatives and pilot programs. The urban affliction will respond only to the sound surgery and humane therapy of a dedicated generation. If our social problems are great, so are our resources, our talents, our aspirations. Man's highest hopes, his most remembered experiments in living, have been acted out in cities throughout the course of history. The future of this nation can be no greater than the future of the American city.

3. Population: Less Is More

"It is possible to hope against hope for many things—that science may learn how to provide us with an unending supply of synthetic foodstuffs, that intelligence and good will may solve all our economic and political problems—but no human agency can increase the surface area of the earth. If the effects of overcrowding on rats can be as deleterious as experiments have shown them to be, what can we expect will happen to human beings?"
—W. H. AUDEN

The contemporary international overpopulation problem is not confined to privation and despair in the world's have-not regions. Though there have been significant favorable population trends in some of the prosperous countries, population pressure continues to be the paramount impediment to an environment that will promote life-enhancing opportunities in all nations.

The ancient and once essential admonition "Be fruitful and multiply" is, in an era of extending life spans and decreasing death rates, a disastrous doctrine. It is a cruel irony that a concept which once assured tribal survival and family security now thwarts the potential of human life.

One of the main obstacles to the advance of a humanizing civilization is the perpetuation of mores that are no longer relevant. Unwise, uncontrolled human increase is deplenishing, not replenishing, the earth. The tyranny of overpopulation is cheapening life, lessening the importance of the individual, and aiding the forces that erode the human soul.

Not long ago, an eminent clergyman summed up the paradox of our postwar public philanthropy in these words: "In the last ten years we have increased human hunger by feeding the hungry. We have increased human suffering by healing the sick. We have increased human want by giving to the needy. . . . The truth of it comes as a shocking discovery, for we have all been brought up in the Christian tradition in which caring for the least of our brethren has been counted the highest virtue. . . . If we are to export life-giving goods and knowledge, we have the moral obligation to export the population-controlling knowledge we also possess."

We have misled the have-not nations and deluded ourselves with the smug assumption, so assiduously cultivated by some scientists and planners, that research will find new sources of food to supply the teeming billions of tomorrow. Research tells us there are vast pastures of unharvested protein in the oceans, and that water desalination may unlock the productivity of the desert rimlands bordering the seas. Optimistic claims for the new technologies of food production, however, have obscured our failure to combat the immediate consequences of overpopulation, and have masked the ultimate impossibility of matching infinite population growth with finite resources.

New technologies notwithstanding, the world food crisis was more acute in 1968 than it was in 1960—or in 1860, for that matter. It is estimated that two-thirds of the people of the world (some millions of them Americans) suffer from hunger, malnutrition, or both. In the face of this, we can no longer cling to the old illusion that rapid population increase is beneficent for man. We should cease the pretense that science will ride to the rescue with easy, early solutions to the problem. As of this moment, the only meaningful solution is a program to halt the heedless increase of human numbers. We can double the productivity of each arable acre, wring more water from the clouds, and learn to stretch our finite resources to their limit, but these achievements will improve the lot of the have-not billions only if irrational population growth is arrested—and soon. The race between production and reproduction cannot be won by turning to increased production alone. It is instructive to contemplate the fact that Japan is the nation that has had the most successful birth-control program in the world for more than a decade and has also enjoyed the highest economic growth rate in the world. It is equally instructive to know that the Aswan Dam has given Egypt, which has no such control program, far more farmland but no increase whatsoever in its ratio of acres of irrigable land to inhabitants.

Precisely because of its devastating economic effect, uncontrolled population growth is the most serious long-term threat to world order. In the past, nations chose war, or had it thrust upon them, to settle power struggles, boundary disputes, demands for lebensraum, or neurotic national pride. Today the widening gap between the have and have-not nations is threatening an imbalance that could destroy the basis of whatever degree of international order man has been able to achieve. If the legitimate expectations of the new nations are frustrated, if optimism is extinguished, then before this century is out a ground swell of disorder could propel to power desperate men who

43

will court holocaust as a supposed means of "starting over again" on this planet. The proven capacities of technology make it possible for relatively underdeveloped states to contemplate inexpensive atomic weaponry. This ominous development, taken with the snail's pace of effective international nuclear-arms control, presents a volatile mix of elements that makes population control the most crucial part of any long-term program of peace-keeping. We must believe that stabilized national growth, based on social freedom and justice, is the best antidote to war. The facts are incontrovertible: sound domestic development can be built only on a rational population policy, and without such a policy, economic and social planning will be at the mercy of the dictatorial pressures released by unlimited human fecundity. A good future depends upon the world's recognition that overpopulation is inimical to progress in the underdeveloped regions of the earth. Overpopulation, the uninvited legislator, will cast a decisive vote in every parliament and sit at all the council tables with the power to ruin the best plans and confound the most adroit diplomacy.

But what of the *have* nations and the pervasive threat overpopulation poses to the quality of everyday existence in such countries? It is clear that the effects of headlong growth are still largely ignored by the more advanced nations. For them the problem does not immediately threaten survival. Nor does it evoke alarm, for the "starvation" it produces has nothing to do with famine and malnutrition. Indeed, its very existence is denied, in the United States especially. Most Americans still react sharply to the notion that we should worry about population increases. Orthodox ideas of the goodness of growth have such a tight grip on the American mind that the suggestion that this generally affluent nation faces any kind of a

44

population crisis is treated as a virtual heresy. We are a large-continent country, it is asserted, and "have plenty of room for growth." Besides, future power and prosperity will depend on rapid growth. Thus the argument goes.

In 1968 some demographers blithely predicted that there will be three hundred million Americans well before the year 2020, and probably a billion by 2080. Most government experts and business analysts uncritically and unquestioningly accept this assumption as a major premise for national planning. This gospel of growth not only permeates all planning, but also makes us automatically acquiesce in a doubling and redoubling of population. So widespread is this state of mind today that it is taken as a fact of life, like the cycle of the seasons or the inevitability of elections; it is as American as apple pie and ice cream. During most of our history it was practical enough. To fill the land and farm it, to build cities and industries, to increase trade and move products and produce throughout the country, and beyond, meant that more and more hands were needed to do the work of nation-building. Nothing about the future smelled of foreclosure, of lack of room, of a need to hold back. And this belief in the necessity of growth remained true of the American mind in spite of the sudden economic squalls, panics, and depressions that have punctuated our history. Development was left to what Kenneth Boulding has called "the vast, incoherent, ecological forces of the market." While this had its social costs, the country survived and thrived. What is important is that this experience of expansion, of high birth rates in a restless native population, and in the incoming tide of millions of European immigrants, implanted, confirmed, and constantly refueled the deep belief that growth was and ought to be the American gospel and that the country was large enough to support any expansion as long as

Americans were willing to work hard to sustain it. To suggest that there could be too many Americans was to invite suspicions not only of one's faith in democracy and of one's patriotism, but also, perhaps, of one's sanity.

This outworn and dangerous growth gospel must be rejected. To bid good-by to it will not be easy. It has in it all the buoyant confidence and open richness of our past. But the farewell must be said, for it has become the chief obstacle to our social, and hence personal, aspirations. We will not build great cities or create an environment commensurate with our needs and our wealth unless we slow down and learn the difficult, demanding arts of graceful, balanced growth.

There is an authoritative indication that we may have begun the deceleration process, though it cannot be attributed to a conscious national decision based on a rational population policy. It is what amounts to a minority report by a distinguished demographer who dissents from the conventional conclusions of most of his colleagues, especially those within the federal government. In 1968, Dr. Donald Bogue, of the University of Chicago, said that it was "absurd" to suggest that it was inevitable that the population of the United States would be three hundred million in thirty-two years—that is, by the end of the century. His much more optimistic prediction, based on the sharp trends of the past few years, is that the year 2000 will find the country with a population stabilized at about two hundred and twenty million. If true, Dr. Bogue's projection is a sign of national sanity. It is not to suggest that he is or might be wrong—*but that he must be made to be right*—to emphasize that his projection, like all demographic projections, assumes certain statistical trends over a long future. What gives necessary pause in Dr. Bogue's welcome forecast is that, while it is undoubtedly based on

sound samplings of live births in statistically valid demographic periods, the births themselves were not events
produced within the framework of a national population
policy, but, rather, were unforeseen responses (chastened
or not by birth control, world uncertainties, and personal
economic assessments) to our traditional gospel of growth.
There's the rub—and it is hard to know how seriously to
take Dr. Bogue's prediction, even as we welcome it with
relief, and are heartened also by the tentative assurance of
statistics indicating that the younger generation has begun
to reject the conventional idea of continuous big-family
growth. It is harder still to know how to reconcile traditional American views of individual liberty and privacy
with a rational population policy for the country. But such
reconciliation is essential to our future, and not at all at
variance with the generally accepted understanding that
the common good is transcendent in a great democracy.

In any event, everything in our contemporary character
still reinforces the growth gospel. We are still held in
thrall by the idea of growth for its own sake. This being
the case, the success we are able to achieve now and in the
future in our human engineering becomes supremely important. We have no rational choice, therefore, but to
search for solid answers to these elemental questions:

Is there an optimum population, an ideal land-people
ratio, for our continent?

What environment—what balance between the works of
nature and the works of man—is most to be desired for the
future?

What manner of cities should we create? How best can
we conserve the countryside? What distinctive elements of
our national life and national estate are worth preserving?
And how shall we preserve them?

What combinations of goods, services, occupations, and

47

amenities will be most apt to promote the prosperity of the human spirit?

These are questions we must ask out of desperate, yet creative, concern for our nation's future. The quality of American life for generations to come will rest on the philosophical and pragmatic insight of our answers.

Yet our most distinctive trait—frontier individualism—has caused us to abhor planning; the finest current plans are honored more by breach than by observance. Such planning as there has been is neither man-centered nor quality-of-life centered. Our land-use policies and our decisions concerning transportation and the design of cities have been dictated by the short-term economics of the market place and by engineering that is often blind to the most basic human needs. Because the auto industry accepted no responsibility for air pollution and the builders of freeways showed no concern for conservation, it should scarcely surprise us that the climates and landscapes of whole regions have been sacrificed to galloping growth.

An increasing gross national product has become the Holy Grail, and most of the economists who are its keepers have no concern for the economics of beauty. Those industrial indices of national well-being—auto output, steel production, heavy construction—have become the universal yardsticks of the American advance. We have had no environmental index, no census statistic to measure whether the country is more or less habitable from year to year. A tranquillity index or a cleanliness index might have told us something about the condition of man, but a fast-growing country preoccupied with making and acquiring material things has had no time for the amenities that are the very heart and substance of daily life.

Our environment has not been ruined by the errors or inroads of any single segment of society. Public outrage has been averted because the innumerable pollutants and defacements were not, taken one by one, outrageous. No floods or forest fires or great dust storms warned us of impending bankruptcy. It is hard to say just when San Francisco began to lose its bay, Los Angeles its salubrious air, or New York its lordly Hudson River. There was no cry of outrage. The reason was a spendthrift and subversive one: the common belief that the piecemeal blight of a green and pleasant land was the price we had to pay for progress.

"Progress" in the past was always conducted in an atmosphere of competitive speed. "Get it done!" was the universal American cry. The cost of the "Sooner" syndrome has caught up with us at last. Now the rule must be "Slow down and plan."

Sheer numbers of people are no longer an advantage for the modern nation. American power during the balance of this century will derive more from the qualitative than the quantitative performance of our society. Imaginative research, pioneering in technology, excellence in education, social and cultural creativity, and a larger understanding of the problems of other peoples (made visible in new programs as salutary and exciting as the Marshall Plan, the Fulbright scholarships, and the more recent Peace Corps) — rather than the mere capacity to proliferate—will express our wisdom and our strength.

The old, although much ignored, traffic-safety slogan "Slow Down—and Live" is pertinent to our predicament. The first fruits of a slow-growth population policy would be a quickening of our capacity to build attractive cities, control crime, and create an equal-opportunity society. We are already wasting too much wealth on quick-fix projects that provide at best a temporary respite from yesterday's mistakes.

Inordinate growth in this country is undermining the life of the individual no less than of the social structure itself. Our system must be based on the primacy of the person, on a goal of individual growth that will replace the obsolete goals of gross growth of population and industry and urbanization. But such changes will require that we question the old assumption of American businessmen that high birth rates are a "bonanza for business." The ever-present problems of human overcrowding can no longer be accepted with the satisfying equanimity immediate profits provide.

This argument will not be easily won. "Society will somehow demand controls to keep life bearable," the *Wall Street Journal* suggested airily in a 1967 analysis of what three hundred million Americans by the year 2000 might mean. Yet this is precisely the helplessly smug rationalization that has led to the environmental erosion of twentieth-century America. *The bearable society is a slovenly substitute for a truly good society.* Yet some federal thinkers are advocates of a merely tolerable tomorrow. A Federal Aviation Agency writer recently offered this explanation of the process whereby the public would eventually accept sonic booms as the price of technological supremacy: "Individuals tend to accommodate themselves to an initially disturbing noise once it becomes a pattern of daily life. There are noises today in cities and in small towns that are taken for granted which, if they were introduced as new noises, would cause disturbances for an initial period of time. . . . People living near Air Force bases, where sonic booms are a common occurrence, don't find them unacceptable, and this may be a sound indication that widespread public tolerance will grow as booms become more a part of daily living." This, I submit, is the insidious logic of a different and diminished America. It implies that men must adapt to machines, and not machines to men; production, speed, novelty, progress at any price must come first, and people second, and mechanization should be pushed as far as human endurance will allow.

These are, of course, the basic assumptions of a bearable society. They put a premium on mobility, machine-created comfort, and artificial experience. Those who have this vision of a twenty-first-century tomorrow obviously feel that mechanization is the solvent for all problems of the future—but there is no requirement that their feelings *should* determine the future. Our experience should tell us we must not add new strains and pressures and discomforts to a high-pressure world. Is it right, for example, to let three hundred people, hurtling across the land faster than sound, interrupt the sleep of three or thirty million by sonic booms?

If we pause long enough to consider the age-old question "What is man?" surely we will be able to discover that the task of the new technology is not to make life bearable, but, rather, to create an environment where the meanings and joys of life—and life itself—are daily reaffirmed and renewed. To accept the debasement of merely endurable living conditions is to reject the fullness of existence, to reject the very humanity of man.

Regrettably, a significant segment of the technological community abets our decline into a merely bearable world of teeming billions. Certain brilliant, high-minded gentlemen are so engrossed in the possibilities of engineering techniques, so embedded in their own highly trained incapacity, that they have lost sight of their own species. The imaginative designer Buckminster Fuller, who would build gargantuan geodesic domes over our cities, is a case in point. His great greenhouses would enclose a mechanized man-controlled climate; the stars, the seasons, and the

51

sun would be walled out in a tricky triumph of technology. Air pollution and weather would disappear in a remarkable feat of engineering. Yet I fear these domes would deny the instinct of man to coexist with nature and would deepen his tendency—rare among the higher animals—to foul his own nest. Ingenious as are the geodesic domes to the intoxicated minds of some designers, so are the capsuled skyscrapers proposed by a few space scientists to save urban open space and "simplify" the routine of life. Though it never was built, it is a safe conjecture that the only inhuman building Frank Lloyd Wright ever designed was a mile-high structure. But, undaunted by Wright's failure, space-system designers are ready to demonstrate man's capacity, as it were, to jam all the inhabitants of India into Manhattan Island in clusters of immense and nearly infinite skyscrapers—and thus "solve" the pressing problems of urban congestion.

Such solutions have abstract interest to engineers, but they cannot satisfy those who would like to build a man-centered and nature-surrounded civilization. When will we learn that automated machine-cities can only shrink the human scale and imperil paramount values? Like other exercises in erecting human hives, they reveal the bankruptcy of the engineer's approach to urbanization. The human anthill will suffocate the most precious human attributes. Yet each jump in human density moves us closer to mechanized, antlike solutions. Overpopulation generates forces that will inevitably destroy diversity, defeat individuality, and encourage the worst forms of regimentation. Life is always ambiguous in a world where essentials are rationed and naturalness is unnatural. Once the magic of intimacy is dispelled by elbow-to-elbow egg-crate living, everything from education to recreation will come wholesale; and personal, small-gained things will fade away, and, with them, the very texture of human existence as we have known it.

It is my belief that the struggle against overpopulation in this country is tied indissolubly to the fight to save the world of nature and to make it an irreplaceable part of everyday life. Those who love the land—naturalists, bird watchers, conservationists (call them what you will) —know that in fighting to save the land they are actually fighting to save man himself. Their passion, though often misinterpreted, is nonetheless persuasive. Thoreau's greatness as a naturalist was subordinate to his greatness as the embodiment of a transcendental principle. He knew that the only way to conserve man's highest attributes was to conserve his relationship to his natural environment; that this environment, with its components of untrammeled things, holds the key to happiness. This was his essential wisdom. Walden Pond and his experience there were not ends in themselves, but representative means through which man could discern and celebrate spiritual reality. It is a mistake, therefore, to make a totem of Walden Pond, though such museumization may be necessary to its physical preservation. The contemporary issue is to devise a nourishing and fully complementary balance between man, his works, and nature.

Nature, after all, is the one constant in the firmament; it serves as both anchor and compass for the one creature that fathoms its meaning and mysteries. Those who seek to further man's interests by ignoring his biological imperatives—his deep taproot in the natural world—will always fail to grasp what they are told by the ecologists and nature lovers, who, be they hunters, canoeists, or tenders of gardens, are not defenders of outlandish fringe values but of man's Antaean tie with the earth itself.

While fine creative talents live in—and have lived in—

cities, and find in congestion no inhibition to their genius, it is no accident that so many of our best writers (Emerson, Thoreau, Whitman, Emily Dickinson, Twain, Frost, Faulkner, Roethke, to name but a few) were country people imbued with the validity of country things. They ask us whether we can root ourselves in an asphalt-centered life without fatally cutting the umbilical cord to the land. They make us ponder the human cost if the cities of tomorrow obliterate the lineaments of the American earth. If, in truth, the American character was shaped by an open, expansive, tough-fibered land, this tie cannot be cut without jeopardy to that character.

"Is it not likely," Sherwood Anderson wrote to his friend Waldo Frank many years ago, "that when the country was new and men were often alone in the fields and the forest they got a sense of bigness outside themselves that has now in some way been lost. . . . Mystery whispered in the grass, played in the branches of trees overhead, was caught up and blown across the American (land) in clouds of dust at evening on the prairies. . . . I am old enough to remember tales that strengthen my belief in a deep semi-religious influence that was formerly at work among our people. The flavor of it hangs over the best work of Mark Twain. . . . I can remember old fellows in my home town speaking feelingly of an evening spent on the big empty plains. It had taken the shrillness out of them. They had learned the trick of quiet." A half-century later we have unlearned, and all but lost, the trick of quiet. The disquiets and distempers of a shrill society cry out for the balm and balance of nature. Our national anxiety will not subside because people or machines proliferate, but because an environment that promotes the harmony of men and land is restored. This does not mean that only a rural society is a good society or that men must "go back to the

54

farm." It does mean, however, that we must invent ways for man to retain his partnership with nature even in an urban context.

For a rational nation proud of its scientific prowess, we are remarkably fatalistic about the future. In regard to population there is a strong streak of passive determinism in our attitude. Will we permit the future just to happen, or will we choose the future we prefer? This is the fateful issue of public policy we tend to ignore. If we want a sustaining and vibrant environment, if we aspire to a social and physical setting that enlarges, not narrows, the choices of the individual, then it is clear that each thoughtless increment of population erodes the options of our tomorrows.

The democratic way is the way of rational choice. Yet men cannot really choose unless the consequences of unlimited growth are spelled out for them. The cures and comforts and scientific spectaculars of the postwar period have seemed to reinforce, perhaps incurably, our traditional optimism. "Life is better than ever" is by and large the current, complacent conviction. Before we are finally caught up in the anthill world dangled before us by the supertechnocrats and mechanistic planners, let us at least understand the implications of the environment they would thrust upon us. We can make room for five or ten billion Americans if that would serve either mankind or our national purpose. But the question is: Will it?

Let me offer a personal forecast of the conditions that will prevail in an America of a billion bodies—or a half-billion, for that matter:

An asphalt America will have overtaken and largely obliterated the green America we still know. Engineering will have overwhelmed nature. The design of this new man-made America will, at best, be more functional; at worst, it will be unattractive, overmechanized, and simply inhuman.

The everyday choices of the individual will have been diminished; his freedom of movement, his space for creative play and contemplation, the diversity of his milieu will have been lessened as his big-sky and open-continent freedoms are drastically reduced.

We will have become a glassed-in, domesticated people, and the outdoor ethos of so much of this country will have gradually disappeared.

The face of the land will be cluttered and unclean. Isolated, unspoiled farmlands and seascapes will be far between—and in California (that region so often reputed to be the precursor of all our tomorrows), the farms and orchards and fields will be gone.

Genuine seemliness will be unattainable. Children will, by slow degrees, have learned to accept the noisy, the vulgar, the pretentious and the ugly; moreover, they will have come to countenance as natural conditions of life the shoddy, the crude, and the unkempt.

Silence will have almost expired. Only the hardy few who wander to the farthest shores or walk the paths of winter will find the serenity of the out-of-doors. There will be the ersatz quiet of soundproof rooms, and the solitude we still enjoy today (an elixir of space, aloneness, and the immanence of nature) will be the scarcest amenity and the most lamented of all the glories common to our lost past.

The Brooklyn, Texas, New England, Rocky Mountain, and other regional differences in our people will have disappeared, victims of the overpowering forces of an over-regimented society. An overpopulated America will be, inevitably, a homogenized, lock-step, increasingly conformist country. Fewer and fewer people will really have the feeling of belonging to a special region, of loving a river or wood, or will know the joy of a kinship with the out-of-doors.

The countryside will be flat-faced. Stream valleys, swamps, and estuaries will be filled and paved over as the waste receptacles of an overpeopled land.

All forms of outdoor recreation will be rationed; the freedom to fish, to hunt, to boat, to walk the wilderness will be an occasional privilege, not an everyday right in a land where, paradoxically, leisure will have increased. Limits on outdoor opportunities will have slowly extinguished interest in wild things and open country. City-bound, house-oriented men and women will turn increasingly to glassed-in avocations and to a sedentary spectatorship greater than that which already poses physiological threats stemming from lack of exercise.

The national parks and all beaches and seashores will be severely rationed. The typical "park experience" will be equivalent to a visit to an oversized zoo. The pressure of people will have caused overdevelopment and overregulation, and in more fragile parks the wonders and regimens of nature will simply be trampled on and destroyed.

Unnumbered species of plants and animals, their habitats destroyed, will have disappeared. There will be little fruit left with the taste of the sun still in it, few lonely beaches with the cry of gulls overhead, few places where the call of wild geese still haunts the air. Overpopulation will have driven much wildlife to extinction. Because most larger animals must have a separate habitat, existence in close proximity with man is not possible. The eagle and the elk may have become memories, or rare phenomena of some remnant wilderness banned to man. But weeds will remain, and with them weedy birds and animals such as the rat, the roach, and the starling, who will thrive.

An America of a billion inhabitants will have lost other

choices and amenities: there will be no clean rivers left, and few brooks where one can safely stoop and drink; there will be few mountain fastnesses where only a pine smell permeates the air; many will eat fish flour, but very few will know the taste of brook trout or fresh-caught salmon.

We will thus lose more than elbow room if we race ahead to the billion bodies and bulging cities the demographers passively predict. Experience tells us that life is cheap in China, dear in the deserts, and most ideal in the medium-peopled countries. Overpopulation means the impoverishment of life no matter what level a goods-and-gadgets standard of living attains.

It is impossible to overstate the case for elbow room. It has, in this country, given Presidents and planners a spacious outlook on life; it has given us room for trial and error; it has been an omnipresent wellspring of the vitality that is characteristically American. Thoreau said the land gave man "a larger margin for life"; it made Theodore Roosevelt a leader "with distance in his eyes." The vaunted American traits of independence and initiative have derived, in part, from the expansiveness of our setting. Individualism flourished wherever space gave play to a wide range of alternatives for action.

There is nothing mysterious about this mystique of space. All members of the animal kingdom—including man—thrive best in that milieu which is most life-giving. Pearl Buck may have indulged in overstatement when she observed that "Democracy is impossible in an overpopulated country." However, it is no overstatement to say that the full life, as we think of it today, or as we would like to shape it for tomorrow, is impossible in an overpopulated land.

The inhibitions of old cultures and outdated religious doctrines have slowed the forming of sound priorities for planetary planning. Despite the amazing advance of science, our current approach to human betterment is most unscientific. We have long since perfected the concept of the land's carrying capacity for animals, and we practice the principle of sustained yield in the management of trees and plants. Yet, strangely, we forget the law of a natural balance when we come to man. We have mastered the arts of animal husbandry, we know the life laws of crops and insects, we know how to plan high-yield growth for agriculture. In effect, we have enhanced the future of everything except the over-all future of the human race. We must now identify the carrying capacity of continents, and evolve an ecology for man in harmony with the unfolding ecology of other living things. If we want it, our engineers can double- and triple-deck our freeways and other public facilities and fill the urban sky line with high-rise apartments, but man can never double-deck a park, a forest, a marsh, or a seashore. If man is to be the prince, not the prisoner, of the system, he must evolve an optimum "sustained-yield" concept keyed to human fulfillment. Can we talk seriously of individual excellence in the long run unless we create environmental excellence as well?

The nightmares of overpopulation would subside if we applied the conservation concept to our own kind. What we call conservation is rooted in the needs of man's nature and the inner order of his universe. It puts the future first and expedience second. It makes the fullness of life the overriding objective of all social planning. The conservation of man now demands that we use this well-tested idea of earth stewardship for the betterment of our own species.

Science has made it simple for us to plan the future of

our most precious resource—the human child. Parents can elect through humane contraception to have only those children they want—and wise men and women should want only that number they are psychologically and financially ready to rear. Such readiness must include not only love and the generous gift of time and attention that total parenthood entails, but also the ability in the society the parents inhabit to provide good health care, educational opportunities, and a life in a constructive social setting.

One could contemplate with equanimity life in these United States if American growth rates and growth patterns reflected a mature, purposeful individual and national will. The arrogance of automatic expansionism has left us little time to ask what people are for. We have not interrupted our pace to consider just how human we could become, and how full and cultured our civilization, if we but agreed on long-term aspirations whose attainment depended on reasoned and restrained growth. Would such limited growth be acceptable? I think so. It would be welcome if we knew how favorable its end results would be in our time and our children's.

The bright uplands of a better world will not come into view until we bring population and human planning into balance. I would have no fear for this country's future if we would turn toward creative parenthood and creative education, if we had already established the foundations of an equal-opportunity society and had mastered the exquisite arts of building cities and preserving the countryside.

We have not, however, and the emergency is already upon us. It has been with us so long, in fact, and we are so accustomed to it, that too many of us seem unaware of it. If we are wise, we will memorize and incorporate into our action plans for our third century these essential quality-of-life maxims:

Bigger is *not* better.
Slower *is* faster.
Less *is* more.

II

4. The Growth Gospel: Some Reflections on Jefferson

"We owed it to do, not what was to perish with ourselves, but what would remain, to be respected and preserved thro other ages." —THOMAS JEFFERSON

One cannot view the blights and befoulments of our land, or contemplate the crises of our cities, without turning to the past for answers to two questions: What are the historical roots of these twentieth-century failures? Is there any old wisdom that might point the way to the restoration of our beloved land?

America is like a tree deeply rooted in the ideas and ideals of the Founding Fathers. None was greater than Thomas Jefferson, the farmer-scholar-statesman-architect-educator of Virginia.

In today's turmoil the cynical may ask what the mind and faith of Jefferson have to offer us. What insights for improving the conditions of our cities can we expect from a man who believed, to use Clinton Rossiter's phrase, "that virtue flourished in rural seats and perished in urban streets"? What guidance on making a multiracial society function is to be received from a man who disapproved of slavery but did not wholeheartedly fight to abolish it? What new directions for conservation can be learned from a man who once wrote, "The indifferent state of agriculture among us does not proceed from want of knowledge merely; it is from having such quantities of land to waste as we please"?

Jefferson, for all his soaring vision about man and his inalienable rights, had meager gifts as a prophet of the American future. He did not sense the coming of the Industrial Revolution or foresee the rapid urbanization of his own country, and he failed utterly to realize that a waste-as-we-please resource policy could ruin the nation.

Despite these shortcomings, the spirit of Thomas Jefferson beckons, for it is the spirit of the man—his youthful, optimistic belief in the improvability of the human condition—that challenges us today. We should not be harsh on the sage of Monticello. When he died in 1826 we were a pastoral people, the "irrepressible conflict" had not been joined, the rivers ran clear, the only smoke was wood smoke, and every defeat for nature was, in fact, a victory for settlement.

The beliefs that shaped nineteenth-century America were deeply imprinted on the American mind by 1826. They included a deep dedication to individual liberty and individual effort as the secrets of success, the belief that all "internal improvements" were desirable, that all growth was good, and the overpowering conviction that the resources of the continent were infinite. The confidence in individual initiative was combined with intense co-

operation and group associations to produce equally necessary elements vital to progress in an undeveloped
country. It was this matrix that shaped the dominant creed
of Jefferson's time. Its elements were:

a belief in the efficacy of unlimited individualism (except for the Negro and the Indian) as a sufficient guide to
growth;

a belief that the resources of the nation were inex-
haustible;

a belief in the future of an agricultural society of small
landowners that ultimately would give each settler a start
and a stake in the United States;

a belief in unlimited population growth (because each
incoming immigrant or new child enlarged both the labor
force and the nation) .

Everyday life confirmed the soundness of these convictions. The America Thomas Jefferson envisioned in his
characteristic maturity was an Arcadia of small farms, a
nation thinly and evenly settled by small freehold farmers
who were the "chosen people of God." The United States
was, moreover, the New World's answer to an Old World
of kings and serfs and cities where life was so congested
men "ate each other."

Thus was the gospel of growth ordained for the newest
nation. As long as the agrarian tradition continued, Jefferson's idyll was both sound and secure. The scattered communities were close-knit. The self-reliance and economic
strength of the family unit were the keys to progress.
Wealth was largely produced by hand and quite evenly
distributed. Even the most aggressive individual, armed
with ax, gun, or plow, could do little harm to the common
resources of the new nation.

So it was from such a base that a great raid on the continent's resources was launched. It started quietly, at first

by men carrying traps. It became ever louder and more destructive as machines were invented. It can be charted in American literature by contrasting James Fenimore Cooper's *The Pioneers* (1823) with Sherwood Anderson's *Poor White* (1920). This ravaging of natural resources would level three-fourths of the forests, drive wildlife to the wall, and "use up" much of the finest soil before the century was through.

The flaws in the gospel of growth so plain, practical, and good to Jefferson and his contemporaries did not appear until the invention of machines, which invaded the agrarian dream, opened the doors to heavy industry, and released forces that were to make large cities inevitable.

Now narrow, individualistic action took on ominous dimensions as a few hyperaggressive persons, driven by the scent of machine-created wealth, carved out personal empires, changed the face of the nation, and destroyed the basis of an equalitarian rural life. An orgy of growth saw new cities, new industries, new means of transportation spring up almost overnight. Here, indeed, was progress, but progress at a price. It had depleted resources, resulted in slovenly cities, and oppressed the working class before its first, frantic phase ran its course. Near the turn of the century, the outlook of the masters of the new industrial age was tersely summarized by two of its typical spokesmen. To a Congressional colleague who argued the case for preserving resources for the future, the Speaker of the House curtly snarled, "Why do we owe anything to posterity? What has posterity done for us?" The owner of the richest railroad met criticism of the social harm of his business practices with a long-remembered contemptuous reply: "The public be damned!"

Well before the nineteenth century was out, the world of Jefferson had been profoundly altered and his ideals

68

were endangered. The young and ebullient Walt Whitman, who rhapsodized in 1856 that "The American compact is altogether with individuals," was brought in old age to doubt whether the democratic idea itself was not imperiled by the monopoly power of the nation's new rulers. The first inning of our Industrial Revolution would have angered and aroused Thomas Jefferson, as would the continued political, social, and economic disfranchisement of the Negro after emancipation. The expanding pattern of poor stewardship of the nation's natural wealth would also have evoked the concern of the man who sent Lewis and Clark to explore the Western lands.

He doubtless would have understood and applauded the muckrakers who aroused indignation over the "malefactors of great wealth," the shame of the cities and the dehumanization of their inhabitants. He would have approved those land-loving Presidents of the twentieth century who fought to reserve a superb estate of scenic and forest and wildlife lands for posterity and who sought successfully to reclaim arid lands, conserve water, save soil, and preserve wild lands and unspoiled seashores for future generations.

But he would also have seen, along with the successes of selective resource conservation, the demeaning defeats administered to man's environment by the more subtle second phase of industrial development. Cities became congested and unclean; air pollution hung like a pall over the large metropolitan areas; most rivers became open sewers, and man-made wastes and poisons entered and interrupted the intimate cycle of life itself.

Having outgrown the Myth of Resource Superabundance nurtured so long and so fatally, we soon developed a new Myth of Scientific Salvation, persuading ourselves that the fouling of our own nest could be quickly cleansed by a sorcerer's apprentice from the house of science. Our popu-

69

lation, meanwhile, doubled between 1915 and 1968, which more than doubled the problems of keeping urban areas habitable.

As we begin to approach our 1976 bicentennial we are, it is to be hoped, approaching the end of a disastrous cycle of abuse. The conclusion is inescapable that spoil-and-move-on "progress" has failed abysmally. There are no more unspoiled places to claim, clear, and settle. The movement to flee from the blighted central cities and build houses on the farms and in the orchards of the hinterland has resulted in undisciplined sprawl into the remaining fresh fields of the countryside and has spread metropolitan debris across the land. The foresight needed to create garden cities within our now limited land resources has not been forthcoming.

What, then, can we learn from Jefferson, who loved the land, defended liberty, and had an unshakable faith in the improvability of the human mind?

He tells us, first, to respond always to change by altering our own instruments of social control: ". . . laws and constitutions must go hand in hand with the progress of the human mind. As that becomes more developed, more enlightened, as new discoveries are made, new truths discovered and manners and opinions change, with the change of circumstances, institutions must advance also to keep pace with the times." And he, who believed so passionately in the freedom of the individual, would remind us once more that ". . . all men are created equal." This famous phrase means for us today that we must provide authentic equality of opportunity. The task is Jeffersonian, unbelievably difficult—and inescapable.

Jefferson, I believe, would urge us not only to accept cities, but also to love their lineaments and strive, by em-

70

ploying our best talents, to make them the finest monuments of our civilization.

He might examine our practices of resource husbandry and remind us that to grow right a nation should grow slowly, and that we must always be cognizant that our wealth in land and our wealth in people are inseparable.

Above all, the life and mind of Jefferson stand unalterably as examples of the capacity of man to develop his own tomorrows, and not merely to let the future happen.

III

5. Project 76: The Urban Answer

"We will never bring disgrace to this our city, by any act of dishonesty or cowardice in the ranks; we will fight for the ideals and sacred things of the city, both alone and with many; we will revere and obey the city's laws and do our best to incite a like respect in those above us who are prone to annul or set them as naught; we will strive unceasingly to quicken the public's sense of civic duty, thus in all these ways we will transmit this city not only not less, but greater, and more beautiful than it was transmitted to us."

—THE ATHENIAN OATH

Anyone in search of solutions to the urban agony must begin with an awareness that our 1968 ideas of "housing" and city renovation are Lilliputian compared with our capacity. We plan and act on a vast scale when it comes to space and defense. But by some obscure alchemy our will is feeble when attention turns to the blighted urban areas where most of us live. It is tragic that at this very moment we are using only a small fraction of our technological prowess on problem-solving in the cities.

But the future is promising, because we will have the resources to achieve an American renaissance. Through continuous sound management of the economy, our annual gross national product should rise above the two trillion level within two decades. Unless false objectives cause us to use our extra wealth on illusory arms races or dubious military actions, or on idle displays of conspicuous consumption, we can achieve goals heretofore beyond the horizons of our hopes. The question is not one of national wealth and resources. These we have. The question is, rather, one of a national will and the formation of a common commitment to great civilizing goals.

In the 1940's the nation organized and successfully carried out the Manhattan Project, which built the atomic bomb. It was accomplished in secret; the basic decision involved only the President and a handful of national leaders; limitless funds were made available and no public accounting was required—a significant departure from normal procedure in a democracy. In the mid-1950's the Congress authorized and the President approved the forty-one-thousand-mile interstate highway system which the New York *Times* a decade later editorially described as: ". . . the most enormous public works project in the history of the world. In cost, it is likely to exceed $60 billion by the time it is completed in 1972. In size and complexity it dwarfs all of mankind's previous engineering works such as the Pyramids, the Great Wall of China, the Panama Canal, or Grand Coulee Dam. . . . As neighborhoods are sliced in two and cemeteries are relocated, neither the quick nor the dead are safe." In the 1960's, all our restless energy, our competitive spirit, and our scientific and industrial prowess were brought into sharp focus in order to put U.S. spacemen on the moon on a predetermined schedule. One point of these three projects is inescapably made: big goals require big plans and clear-cut deadlines to achieve success.

A nation that could organize and carry out such dominating projects can, in the 1970's, genuinely begin the even more difficult and urgent task of transforming the worst slums from Manhattan to Los Angeles into civilizing habitats for man. Technicians who can construct spacecraft that circle the earth in an hour can also help us build balanced cities. If we have the expertise to engineer the largest system of highways in history, we should also be able to assemble teams of specialists who can build bridges between the races that have lived on, but never really shared, this continent for over three centuries. Once we apply American science, strength, and social knowledge to the shortcomings of our society, we may discover that domestic progress which cleanses our country of malice and builds a life-giving environment for all of our citizens is the most effective foreign policy that we can possibly devise for the future.

The two chief failures that confront us as we approach our bicentennial—a failure to build livable cities and a failure to eradicate racism—are failures to establish genuine democracy. We have amassed awesome destructive power, but our cities are a mess. We have acquired the material trappings of great wealth, but have still to exhibit the wisdom that will build good will between groups. Yet the mark of a mature civilization is always made in the twin realms of culture and human understanding. Do we have the determination, the wisdom, and the will to redirect the revolution of science and technology that has produced this power and wealth and to use our combined gifts to transform life in this country? This is the crucial question.

We cannot answer in the affirmative unless we first realize the dangerously small dimensions of our existing efforts and expectations. Two decades of "urban renewal" have improved less than one per cent of the urban blight in this country. Today we have ten million substandard

77

units of housing. Postwar public-housing and slum-clearance projects have not kept pace with the rising demand for low-cost housing and the rapid obsolescence of jerry-built structures of earlier years. Our lenient local tax and enforcement policies, moreover, still reward inaction by the owners of slums. The remedies we have applied to our urban ills have largely consisted of dabbing disinfectant on selected sores, not in the bettering of the lives of all citizens. Even the most successful exercises in downtown renovation—in such cities as Hartford, Baltimore, San Francisco, Philadelphia, and Fresno—stand today only as glistening ornaments in teeming seas of decay. It is a discouraging commentary on our ingenuity that we waited until the mid-1960's to try out, on much too small a scale, such promising ideas as President Johnson's rent-supplement and "Model Cities" programs. We must now recognize that piecemeal approaches to renovation have failed to meet the fundamental challenge. They are invariably inefficient, often inequitable, and have all the shortcomings of patchwork repair.

Plans of action of a large scope are needed to reach and take full advantage of economies and to upgrade the quality of life in all of our cities. The task is less to renovate than to re-create. More than slum clearance is involved. There are gilded as well as slum ghettos. Given the will, we can turn our drab urban landscape into a spiritually nourishing as well as physically satisfying environment, not only in a broken Newark or a gutted Detroit, but also in ugly cities, towns, and villages that stretch from New York to Memphis and on to Los Angeles.

The parsimony of our imagination and planning is visible at every turn. When they attempt to grapple with desperate issues, enlightened mayors like John Lindsay and Jerome Cavanagh have no choice but to apply tourniquets and hope for help from Washington. It is both demeaning and self-defeating when mayors call for ninety-to-ten federal matching money as a cure-all to their own pressing problems while at the same time they resist undertaking other far-reaching measures. For example, when the big-city mayors opposed the "new towns" incentive provision of the Housing and Urban Development Act of 1965, this promising approach to urbanization was stricken from the bill. The mayors' attitude was based on the belief that new towns would siphon off the "best" citizens and the most profitable new industries, leaving the existing cities with heavier welfare rolls and unemployment. The best-conceived new towns would not only relieve the population pressure-cooker of the biggest cities, but could create model patterns of fully integrated housing as well.

It was disheartening in the summer of 1967 when the realities of Vietnam priorities and the mood of a balky Congress forced a concerned Vice-President of the United States within a few hours to temporarily abandon his call—made as Detroit smoldered—for a "Marshall Plan" for American cities. Hubert Humphrey was basically right. We *do* need a vast program, equal not only to the dimensions of the problems but also to the capacities we possess. We must have a wholesale overhaul and dramatic action that will produce reforms. But for that action to occur we require something that will quicken the conscience and excite the expectations of the entire nation.

The hard-hitting Kerner Commission "Report of the National Advisory Commission on Civil Disorders" failed for two principal reasons to galvanize action. First, the high cost of the Vietnam war foreclosed immediate consideration by a Congress reluctant to approve even a war-financing ten-per-cent tax surcharge urgently requested by the President. Second, the Commission's proposal for "crash" efforts in the areas of jobs, housing, education, and welfare at "unprecedented levels of funding" ran head on into the pervasive anti-big-city bias of the Congress. It must be remembered that the central cities, with their urgent human needs, contain only a small fraction of our total voting population. Almost eighty per cent of our people reside in the suburbs, moderate-sized cities, and the rural regions of the nation. Or, to put it another way, four-fifths of the members of the House represent citizens who reside in communities other than the sixty-one cities of 200,000 or more. This is not a criticism of the excellent work of the Kerner Commission, but, rather, of its necessarily narrow scope. The Commission was directed by the President to concentrate its attention on the human causes of unrest in the ghettos of the largest cities. Even so, its limited prescription failed to move either the Congress or the country, because the only way to arouse and involve the nation is by a strategy to rebuild the entire nation, not simply to redo its most blighted parts; it did not spark a national response because it failed to look beyond the big-city ghettos toward the unfinished work of a half-finished society. We need a strategy and a plan that, while giving first priority to slum eradication, will have a further range of priorities to transform our communities and our lives. There is in our country still too much bigotry and too little altruism for even the piecemeal program prescribed by the Kerner Commission to gain the support it will need for full implementation.

The experience of the 1960's tells us that "wars" on poverty and slums will continue to receive halting, underfunded support unless we have the imagination to attack these ills in the much larger context of expansive aims and goals capable of regenerating the whole nation. We must view these ills as a crisis of opportunity. The considerable problem now is to broaden and go beyond the Kerner Commission's recommendations, to include the whole nation, and thereby to enlist the interest of all Congressmen and every citizen. More piecemeal plans geared to quantitative conventional programs—more jobs, better schools, improved welfare, accelerated housing—will not arouse the nation. We need a dream of excellence and betterment to involve and excite every citizen.

We have not succeeded in this century in devising William James's moral equivalent of war because we have never dared to think and act on a scale that would involve each individual and every community across the land. Franklin Roosevelt turned the Great Depression into an opportunity to build sorely needed public works, to replant forests, to harness the hydroelectric power of our great rivers. Unhappily, these depression-combating programs had to give way to wartime priorities, then to postwar catching up on consumer goods and an unplanned rush of construction and production that has left every city in this land from New York to Nome with its poor, its slums, its outworn public services, its social diseases, its disordered environments.

We need now, not a call to cure specific diseases, but a plan to make all cities cathedrals for everyday existence. We need:

a plan that envisions full employment as the humane use of human beings, not merely more jobs;

conditions that will create social health and shrink the need for welfare, not merely "improved" administration of "increased" welfare programs;

balanced cities, not merely more housing;

liberation from the congested prison of private wheels by the creation of fast and quiet public transportation.

81

A sound political base, not altruism, should be relied on to accomplish these things. The watchwords of the program should be "opportunity" and "quality." To meet the art-of-the-possible test of politics, our approach must tackle rural as well as urban renewal, and be as concerned with conditions in Indian hogans as in the barrios of East Harlem. It should be as interested in the revitalizing of small towns as in the renovation of the largest megalopolis. It should expend as much creative thought on the refurbishing of middle-sized cities as on the reconditioning of New York or Chicago, and contemplate the erection of many comely new towns as well.

Were we to decide that urban revival will be our dominant ambition for the remaining years of this century, this establishment of a national priority would not be without precedent in our history. The federal government made agriculture its first priority during most of our history. It granted huge slices of the public domain to railroad promoters to improve our systems of transport, and smaller slices to the land-grant colleges. Priority was later given to the restoration of the Tennessee Valley when it lay in ruins. In the 1940's first priority went to winning the war; in the 1950's, to highway-building; and in the 1960's the space mission to the moon was our big adventure.

Pilot programs and peripheral "wars" on social problems will never suffice as a moral equivalent of war, however. We need a task so spacious, a goal so intimate yet universal, that our people will be unified by the endeavor it compels. We need a plan that will enlist all segments and cities of America, and become the most exciting national enterprise since the founding of the republic.

In 1976 we will reach what could be the most notable milestone of this century: the two hundredth anniversary of the declaration that began the United States of America.

If we elect to be conventional, we will celebrate this event with a world's fair in a selected city (as we did at Philadelphia on our centennial in 1876). Or, as this book proposes, we can commemorate our bicentennial with a more significant undertaking: we can begin a temple-building enterprise of our own, a vast project *to make all our cities fair, and all our human relations amicable.* It could be called "Project 76."

Every genuine civilization reaches an apogee when it feels secure against attack, and, possessing sufficient wealth and talent, enters into what one might call the temple-building phase of its history. In most cases this moment of maturity has coincided with a flowering of the human spirit. When fleets and frontiers are temporarily unthreatened, there is time to contemplate the consummations of culture; men may attempt to express an age in stone, in vast engineering projects, or in exalted cities. In the past, the Golden Age of Greece, the summit decades of the Roman Empire, the cathedral-building impulse of the Middle Ages, the Italian Renaissance, and Elizabethan England represented multifaceted heights of cultural consummation. The ruins and monuments and engineering works one can inspect today at Persepolis, Jarash, Athens, Rome, Florence, Paris, and London are landmarks of the Western world's all too rare expressions of man's exaltation. The roads, aqueducts, temples, churches, theaters, triumphal arches, fountains, boulevards, statues, and amphitheaters bespeak the gifts and goals of these societies; the forms and spaces and amenities they designed, the environments they developed as habitations for man, throw light on their dreams—and on our possible ambitions, not for an elite, but for all men.

The citizens of a seminal democracy cannot afford, as the oligarchs of earlier civilizations could, to settle for a shining capital or to construct a few exemplary cities. Ours is a society of many needs, potentials, and mansions; our only legitimate aims must encompass all cities of all sizes and attempt to enhance the well-being of every inhabitant.

Ideally, Project 76 would be formulated by a commission of eminently talented citizens called to a keynote conference organized by the President in 1969 to discuss "The Agenda for the Third American Century." This conference should be given more care and prestige than any previous White House conference, including Theodore Roosevelt's Conservation Conference of 1908. The entire leadership community of the nation—including the Congress—should be invited to participate. To ensure a nonpartisan consensus, the President should wisely remain in the background. He should urge the creation of a vast and viable program that could win and sustain the nation's enthusiasm. The commission itself should devise detailed goals, priorities, and realistic budgets to permit the program's completion before the year 2000. Once endorsed by the states and cities, and authorized by the Congress, the action timetables and appropriations schedules should be accorded stronger support than our highway and space programs have received.

The first phase of Project 76 should involve every community in drafting a master plan to achieve the redesign and renovation of its entire environment no later than the year 2000. Each mayor could convene a "Council to Recreate the City" whose dynamic, representative, revolving membership would educate the community, review all individual projects, and gear future plans to aims of excellence. For the first time, decisions about design and the harmonizing of private actions and public amenities could be guided by the finest thought and leadership in each city. This would initiate a continuing and creative dia-

84

logue between artists, designers, leaders of labor, business, and the professions, politicians, and the people. "Developers" would no longer decide the shape of the city, but would be forced to consider fresh solutions in which present and future welfare would be interwoven. This could give to the public life of many communities a creative excitement largely unknown in this country. The best ideas of artists and designers would filter into the public consciousness and improve everyday life. Imaginative plans would incorporate all the arts; there would be a flowering of opportunities for engineers, architects, sculptors, muralists, painters, landscape architects, and local leaders of culture and recreation. Every city could not be expected to produce a Henry Moore, an Orozco, or an Eero Saarinen—but some might!

To succeed, Project 76 would have to be truly national. It would offer the same promise of rural renewal as of urban renovation. To gain unswerving Congressional support, it should encompass every community of every size from Miami to Hilo, from Aroostook to Anchorage.

The master-planning phase could begin immediately, with federal grants to cover at least half the cost, and with local public and private participation supplying the balance. Each community should have a plan and some large-scale projects underway by 1976. Project 76 should reject the project-by-project approach in favor of planning addressed to the total environment of entire regions. It should build on the best experience of the public-housing, urban-renewal, rent-supplement, and Model Cities programs of the past, but it should demand that each of these efforts be part of a comprehensive master plan. Washington could co-ordinate the national goals and guidelines, but all physical and social blueprints should be formulated and executed by local leadership. While initial planning

85

was proceeding during the first two or three years, immediate priority should be given to the job-creating clean-up work, which could be done by the hard-core unemployed in the worst slums. Just as Franklin Roosevelt sent unemployed youths into the devastated woodlands to replant the forests, we should launch an urban clean-up corps to roll back blight, reclaim public beauty, and begin the training of the work force required for large-scale blight-removal projects.

Federal planning and construction grants for urban renewal and community facilities should be trebled to five billion the first year. That first year we should spend at least as much on Project 76 as we have been spending annually on the exploration of outer space. Such expenditures should be increased, out of our constantly expanding gross national product, to an annual grant level of fifty billion dollars no later than 1985. The federal government should deal directly with the cities. Funds could be channeled to them under a distribution formula giving a first-phase priority to slum renovation, but guaranteeing ultimate participation by each community on the basis of its population and willingness to invest matching money (perhaps twenty per cent) in Project 76 programs. As the action accelerated, solutions for such regional problems as the providing of mass transit for each megalopolis, the encouragement of new towns in appropriate areas, and the renewal of towns and cities of under thirty thousand in population (to slow down the implosion of people into the big cities) should get special attention.

Some skeptics will assert that we lack the talent and skill to plan the renovation of a whole country. I believe there are more gifted designers and design-oriented citizens within the gates of our several cities than we realize. The experience of Montreal with Expo 67, of San Antonio with

HemisFair, and of St. Louis with its Jefferson Expansion Arch tells us that big plans which excite a community will uncover the men and the money needed to make brilliant solutions feasible. Montreal did more than prepare a national fair for Canada. It built the most handsome, restful subway system in North America, and restructured much of its core city as well. As the chosen torchbearer of Canadian excellence, Montreal turned an anniversary celebration into an opportunity to make itself a staging area for experiments in the large-scale recasting of a city. Expo itself demonstrated that good design, related to the reason for the city's being, is the *sine qua non* of real progress, complements industrial efficiency, and can have an inspiring effect on a whole people. By contrast, the 1964–65 New York World's Fair had as its primary goal commercial gain, the plans were fragmented, and the painful and profligate results did practically nothing to improve living standards or spiritual tone in troubled New York.

Other communities and leaders—Hartford and its insurance executives, Mayor Lawrence and the Mellon family of Pittsburgh in the 1940's, Victor Gruen and the downtown merchants of Fresno—have perceived that bold plans to restructure the core city, and a concern for quality, do succeed in giving a health-restoring lift to city life. Our need now is to learn the lessons of Montreal, St. Louis, Hartford, Pittsburgh, San Antonio, and Fresno and translate them into an exciting Project 76.

Our universities and design professions constitute pools of talent no less gifted than the unheralded Canadian team that put Expo together. To rebuild our cities with style and distinction will require interdisciplinary teams of architects, engineers, sociologists, anthropologists, economists, lawyers, and managers, bound together by a common commitment to the humanizing of the urban milieu.

Project 76 could enable us to assemble unprecedented design teams in all parts of this country. If we dare have faith in the aptitudes and aspirations of our own people—and especially the young generation—we can have a blossoming of American genius and art that would truly transform the face and character of our country.

As a human program, Project 76 would be far more fulfilling than highway construction or triumphs in outer space. After its early work of reclamation and reconstruction, it should move to a middle phase in which the reshaping of our cities would occur. The culmination should occur near the end of the century with the construction of museums, health facilities, theaters, libraries, and centers of art and recreation in all our cities.

Project 76 could influence the whole course of our history. As we have learned in our peacetime experience by carrying out a Marshall Plan and a national adventure in space, any great decision or enunciated goal, if it is a decisive, galvanizing act, has far-reaching consequences. It coalesces thought and energies. It stirs syntheses into being, sets events and investments in motion, all of which give a sense of purpose and commitment otherwise lacking.

To a degree the comparison is unfair, but one is impelled to measure the main benefits of our great national project of the 1960's—space exploration—against the potential of a Project 76 for the 1970's and beyond. Space exploration *is* a great adventure, though not because it gives us the dubious satisfaction of knowing we might win a race with the Russians. There are other advantages, what have been called "spin-off" benefits—to technology, to our understanding of weather, and to the discovery of resources on earth. These gains and discoveries are real and transcend considerations of prestige and scientific supremacy. But, to be honest about it, the space program does not have a major immediate impact on our everyday lives or needs. It has not made our cities more livable. It has not given us new solutions to social problems. One thing it *has* done is prove beyond doubt the prodigious value of total planning, of goal-setting, of multidisciplinary systems analysis and action, and this is the great contribution of the space effort. Let it take us to the moon, but let us apply its techniques and systems approaches to our terrestrial stars—to our cities and ourselves.

An enterprise with the promise of Project 76, by contrast with the space program, but by using its totality of planning, could have a "spin-in" result that would affect the lives of every citizen. The progress of machines in outer space would not cease to captivate us, but we would develop a more compelling interest in the rebuilding of our environment, perhaps by a new triumph of the aerospace industry working with social planners. Spin-in would mean that the hardware we produced would become a permanent capital asset of the nation. All energy and money used to renovate the nation's cities would enter a recycling orbit; each investment would create new wealth and add to the human- and physical-resource base of the nation.

In time, the spin-in of Project 76 could transform the art of living and the opportunity for man's further humanization, with machine power his servant, but never his master. A self-confident society at peace with itself would not need to worry about specious "images"; rather, it would acquire real prestige from once again making this nation "the last, best hope of earth." And having found the right mix of altruism and self-interest, it could make a maximum contribution to world peace and world order. For once, the quality of our example—not the power of our economic thrust—would recommend us.

An additional spin-in effect of incalculable importance would be the challenge to our youth to become the creators of a new America, the excited participants in a revolution that could reshape our society.

As the project unfolded, we could begin for the first time to see our cities not merely as centers of commerce, but as stages on which men and women could act out noble experiments in living. Each advance—each new urban university, each altering of the urban fabric, each new library, each park and playground, each beautiful subway, each introduction of an open square from which a new neighborhood could radiate, each downtown mall or mini-park—would lead to new demands for larger and better solutions. Each humanizing feature of beautification or restoration would make the antihuman features of cities more intolerable.

There would be the prospect that a new generation of civic conservationists will fight for urban beauty and order with the same fierceness the Sierra Club conservers have in their fight to save the wild lands of the nation. They would love the man-made and man-arranged lineaments of their cities—the historic houses, fountains, vistas, stones, bridges, and spires—as much as the naturalist loves nature. They might also develop a man-centered "urban ecology" to ascertain the conditions most conducive to the mental, physical, and spiritual health of the human species. And they might, at last, put the case to the nation that man and his environment, be it the works of man or the works of nature, are an inseparable system, and that the so-called amenities are sustaining wellsprings of life itself.

We would then reject many of the irrational patterns of everyday existence, and open our minds to such proposed innovations as the Embarcadero (the Golden Gateway Centers in San Francisco, where large downtown developments including housing, offices, and commercial stores are cast on a mall elevated over the existing street pattern); the "new towns in town" proposals for the eighteen-hundred-acre National Training School site in Washington, and satellite cities such as Reston, Virginia, and Columbia, Maryland. It will not only be more economical, but also more humanizing for man to live and work and play in settings where life is not car-centered.

Communities could make safety and sanity the norm, where men and children could walk unhurried to work and to school, to see and to touch nature and to rub elbows with people like and unlike themselves. Nothing contributes more to the alienation of the races than our insulated and compartmentalized bedroom suburbs, where we exist side by side with people who share our tax brackets but not our lives. One of the finest new-town ideas is the proximity of housing for diverse income groups, which makes it both appealing and necessary for different races and income levels to serve each other and to share their schools, home life, and leisure. Now that open housing is a national policy, we will find that the intimate interweaving of racial strands will give new scope and strength to our society. Whitney Young was correct when he pointed out recently: "Increasingly it is the insecure, the frightened, the unsure, who need to surround themselves with sameness. But there is richness in diversity and white citizens will benefit just as surely as Negroes."

Once we give up the idea that everyone should be able to drive an auto to everyone's front door, some bold cities can take one giant step that will open up a fantastic set of new options for urbanization. This would occur the moment we elected to regard the publicly owned land now used for streets and alleys as a land bank for people. After all, the asphalt maze can give way to gardens or fountains

91

if we so choose. In the average central city, over forty per cent of the surface area is devoted to streets. In some, such as Houston, the figure exceeds sixty per cent. If even a portion of this space were reclaimed for people as malls, open space, and greensward, it not only would be an outstanding investment in tomorrow but also would open the door to superblock development that could alter the whole face and fiber of our cities. One need only look at Washington, D.C., to see what such space can mean to an urban environment. Yet in Washington itself, if only one-fourth of the street area was reclaimed, the park and open space would be doubled. One-half of the streets could easily carry twice the auto traffic in a central city if sensible parking regulations were adopted and if people, buses, and traffic crosscurrents were separated. Logic points to surface superblocks for people, with high speed and noise underground, and only human-scale movement overhead. Beginnings have been made. Linear City, in Brooklyn, utilizing the air rights above an expressway for housing, shops, and schools, may be a breakthrough. The Pennsylvania Avenue Plan for Washington envisions the closing of several streets to traffic and the use of the liberated space corridors as pedestrian malls and directional focusing vistas to landmarks along the avenue. Nicollet Avenue in Minneapolis has closed the main shopping street to cars and allows only buses.

I would propose as part of Project 76 that upon completion of the interstate highway system at least half of the Highway Trust Fund monies be employed for at least two decades to make our nation's urban transportation systems more humane. These funds could be used to make transportation a creative force in our cityscape. Right of ways could be widened to provide green strips for hiking and bike and bridle trails. Roadways could be placed underground, giving the surface and air rights back to the people. Some expressway locations could provide delightful vistas and visible boundaries to urban segments. Water fronts such as those in New Orleans and San Francisco could be exalted instead of exploited. One need only look at the George Washington Parkway on one side of the present-day Potomac River in our nation's capital and the Whitehurst Freeway on the other to see the difference. The one destroys its water front; the other enhances it.

Each city or region should also develop a larger land bank in the countryside, with authority—in the exercise of foresight—to buy and sell land and interests in land to further the comprehensive plans of the region. Such agencies could serve as a conservation conscience, and a rallying point for swift action to ensure that the highest and best use of all land was achieved. Such a model entity—with broad powers to orchestrate action in the whole river basin—has been proposed for the Potomac by a group of eminent planners. It would be a land-centered T.V.A., and once the "bank's" capital was assured, it would revolve as deposits and withdrawals were accomplished to carry out the purposes of the larger plan.

Our past experience again offers a guide. The reclamation of the arid lands of the West has been an expensive and technically difficult process, but the results are a demonstration of the values achieved when our national attention is focused on a specific problem. Why should we not now apply this experience, and money and prowess, to reclaiming some of the humanly arid lands in our cities?

The Model Cities experiment will soon begin to produce experience and results in the whole spectrum of city-building. This imaginative concept may prove to be the single most significant Great Society program of the 1960's. It could develop into the main vehicle for Project 76, and mark the beginning of many revolutionary planning concepts. Advocacy planning (in which planning teams attempt to ascertain and articulate the ideas of neighborhoods), block grants to local authorities, comprehensive planning involving not only physical but also cultural, economic, and social factors, and the planned sharing of facilities to eliminate costly duplication and to preserve open space will no longer be theories. Consideration of functional, not geographic or political, regions as the basis of planning will be an accepted fact, and when complemented by the New Communities Act of 1968 its effects will be far more universal. Above all, the results will make a majority of the American people reject the idea that mediocrity is inevitable.

Where Project 76 would differ from the Model Cities plan, however, is in scale and scope; it would involve every American and every aspect and horizon of his environment. Project 76 would also have a spin-in effect by acting as a catalyst to encourage each city to protect and enhance its very individuality. Each city, to a degree, has a separate history and unique natural endowments. Competition among American cities might serve to counteract the deadening trend toward alikeness and uniformity. In this, each municipality would strive to conserve and distinguish its landscapes and cityscapes and historic landmarks. Such a creative endeavor would summon the artistic instincts of the whole nation, build local pride, and encourage the diversity and style that are the distinguishing marks of a genuine civilization. Small nations rightly take pride in their tidiness, homogeneity, and in their cameos of history. A continental country should promote and preserve the special flavors, colors, and cultures of its different regions. The special appeal today of Santa Fe, Savannah, San Francisco, New Orleans, and Sitka is the distinctiveness, the indigenous peculiarities prized and kept. Without their respective features—the earth colors, native architecture, trolley cars, totem poles, markets, historic houses, and other landmarks—these cities long ago would have lost their special flair. As we take pains to encourage Vermont and Hawaii to keep billboards off their roadways, so we should urge Lancaster County, in Pennsylvania, to sustain its superb farmscapes, Santa Fe its pueblos, and San Antonio its riverside restaurants and walkways. The fight against eyesores must be paralleled by a fight for authentic tradition.

Hundreds of indistinguishable and therefore undistinguished communities across the country might rediscover their particular character and upgrade their living values by accenting the appeal of unique natural settings, regional climates, and indigenous building materials. As places like Philadelphia, Annapolis, and New Harmony, Indiana, have demonstrated, historical-preservation opportunities exist, in all parts of our land, which can confer style and flavor on large and small cities. If we would only pause long enough to study the human implications of Thoreau's powerful injunction "Simplify, simplify!" many of our communities would imitate Carmel, California, and cultivate uncomplicated natural arrangements and amenities. A special project can also bring life to a community, as it has to Laguna Beach, California, with its Pageant of the Masters (a singular dramatic production that enlists the participation and pride of the entire community), and to Cooperstown, New York (with its Baseball Hall of Fame), and many other creative communities. A tapestry of total excellence will emerge from distinctive efforts to give special distinction to our cities. If, in 1980, we are unable to tell Dallas from Houston or Harrisburg from Omaha, the country will be the poorer for it.

If we care deeply about each decision that can improve or demean the *ambiance* of the city, urban conservationists will be called on to do much more than fight angry skirmishes to save a bay, a marsh, a water front, a riverway, a vista, or a piece of parkland from the faceless "developers." They will begin to be able to win most of the big and little fights for superior solutions to growth problems, and make the stewardship of urban resources a moral imperative of city politics.

This qualitative transition should go hand in hand with a historic shift of political power to the local arena. Project 76 should not only elevate the importance of municipal government; it should also encourage a restructuring of responsibility to make the cities exciting centers of action. If the states delegate much broader power to city hall, and the federal government provides funds at the levels required for Project 76, the reviving of local leadership could be one of the notable chapters of our third century of nationhood. It will be foolish to devise bold plans unless we also renew our political system, making much bolder leadership possible at the city and county level.

With a few notable exceptions, the American city today is not what local leaders consciously have shaped. Entrepreneurs have mounted a piecemeal assault against the cityscape, and most of their activities have demeaned, not enriched, the common wealth of urban America. Land speculation, not indecisive city fathers, has created the face and character of the city. The main fault lies not with the weak leadership which in the past accepted ugliness, congestion, and decay as inevitable, but with a system that denied city hall the power and prestige needed to generate those actions that would transform city life.

The permissive politics of the past, beguiled by the belief that speculative building and freewheeling industrialism were and should be the American way, abdicated the

96

power to control urban design and to protect the quality of living standards. Project 76 should mark the beginning of a partnership politics that will enlist industry, labor, the design professions, elected and unelected community spokesmen, and, most of all, the people themselves in the intimate co-operation needed to reshape whole cities. This will require not only more Mellons and more Mayor Lees of New Haven, but also unprecedented patterns of collaboration that will refresh and redefine every aspect of local politics.

The Project 76 approach will not work unless we are willing to vest new power in local government and attract new leaders to the local scene. It is no accident the most successful U.S. mayors in recent years have been the men who were given extra powers, gained broad community support, and stayed around long enough to complete projects that changed the outlook of a city. To again select a few notable examples, the late David Lawrence (who presided over the partial renovation of Pittsburgh), Richard Lee (who has refurbished New Haven), and former Mayor Raymond Tucker (who removed some of the slums and changed the sky line of St. Louis) were—and are—men who served for more than a decade, who had the complete support of their "leadership communities," and were able to achieve expansive and expensive solutions to urgent problems while insisting on the various "extras" that are the ornaments of handsome cities. They knew, as we must realize, that such expenses are self-amortizing. The real cost is in inaction; there is neither practicality nor economy in ugliness, in decay, in despair, in disorder. "Ugliness," as Vachel Lindsay once observed, "is a kind of misgovernment." It is absurd to talk of "new towns in town" or to have visions of vast projects to supplant slums with handsome neighborhoods unless we intend to give the cities the power and funds to make such projects feasible.

97

Our sick civic governments need both a transfusion of funds and an overhaul of functions to make them the arenas of action they must become.

Montreal, under the inspired guidance of a strong mayor, Jean Drapeau, should be an example to the cities of its neighbor nation. The stunning renovation of the urban core, the Placeville Marie, the building of North America's first new subway in the twentieth century, the brilliant design and execution of Expo 67 raised the quality of life in Montreal to a much higher standard. Strong leadership can transform a metropolis—that is the object lesson of Montreal. Its citizens will not accept mediocre solutions after the experience of Expo.

We have no right to expect an urban American renaissance unless we give fresh power and prestige to our own local leadership. In the past, the measure of a city administration's success has been the number of new jobs created, the new industries attracted, the extent of suburbs annexed, the reduction in the bonded debt. But in the future we should expect our mayors to regard their administrations as failures unless they leave their cities cleaner, more livable, more beautiful, and more alive with warmth and fulfilling cultural and commercial activity.

Once we set our sights on goals worthy of our wealth and technical skill, we will also demand—and get—a different order of pride and performance from the men of business whose choice it is to do much to influence the life of their cities. The spirit of Project 76 would mean we would measure the performance of an electric utility as much by the miles of line put underground, as much by reductions in air pollution, as by the cost to the consumer of its energy; we would judge our road builders more by highways hidden or beautifully landscaped and by the ease and delight they give city travel than by the high speeds they allow or the swath they cut; we would require that all urban land developers "plant" fountains and plazas and parklands and spacious school sites as part of the cost—and opportunity—of doing business in the city of the future.

This would not be an improper intrusion on the prerogatives of private ownership, but an exercise of its responsibility. Already the most enlightened men of business have voluntarily assumed such challenges, convinced that beauty is not only the finest form of advertising, but a sound investment as well. The Seagrams Company gave New York City a stately plaza with fountains. J. Irwin Miller, of Cummins Engine, helped Columbus, Indiana, become "the town that architecture made famous." William Roth brightened San Francisco by restoring Ghiardhelli Square. Insurance companies built the brilliant Constitution Plaza and revived downtown Hartford. William S. Paley gave New York a mini-park. These are only a few isolated examples of business leadership that could become an extended everyday spin-in if we dared get Project 76 underway. The insurance industry has pledged a billion dollars to slum rebuilding. For the future, it could apply the vast power of its mortgage purse to enrich the environment by invariably insisting on quality of design and on an abundance of human amenities.

The Project 76 approach could, then, bring us to a temple-building time of our own, end the deadly and demeaning division between the races, and make the remaining years of the century as honored and remembered as the founding years of the American republic. It could challenge us, at last, to develop a wisdom and a will to match the material wealth and technical skill already at our command. And were such a challenge to succeed, it would unlock the door to the era of greatness that has eluded us for too long.

99

6. New Dimensions of Conservation

"The only real capital of a nation is its natural resources and its human beings. So long as we take care of and make the most of both of them, we shall survive as a strong nation, a successful nation and a progressive nation—whether or not the bookkeepers say other kinds of budgets are from time to time out of balance." —FRANKLIN D. ROOSEVELT
(1938)

The way a people possess the land they live on is always a revealing comment on their character and institutions. The tidy farmscapes of the Pennsylvania Dutch country and the billboardless vistas of Hawaii say something positive about our people, just as dying Lake Erie, the polluted rivers in every industrial state, the poisonous air of Southern California, and the hideous slums of our big cities express the distorted values that permit us to demean and diminish so much of our continent.

Realism requires much more than moralizing about the industrial "rights" and environmental "wrongs" of past years in which, heedlessly, we put profits ahead of the future welfare of all the people. The balanced bookkeeping we are now developing compels us to confront the real cost of our failures and to assign financial accountability and responsibility for action to regions, cities, and industries so that the true capital of America may be reclaimed.

As we enter our third century, conservation must sharply define its concern for specific resources and teach us to realize that plans to protect air and water, wilderness and wildlife are in fact plans to protect man. We will attempt to enhance these resources not simply because it is desirable to have wilderness or wildlife or clean air and water but because such action is essential to the self-renewing systems of nature that sustain the earth.

We can remedy the mistakes of our profligate years not merely by piecemeal actions that attempt to repair the depredations of the past, but also by a permanent, all-encompassing commitment to the wealth-renewal of a husbandry of true thrift. The concept that guides us in the years ahead must equate progress with the fullness of human life. Jefferson once observed that the "land belongs to the living generation." In the limited sense he intended, it does indeed, but the larger trusteeship we must espouse now will seek the creation of an order which not only promotes the well-being of the living, but also enhances the total environment, which is the basic wealth we bequeath the unborn. The folklore of the price system, which inflates the value of today's satisfactions and understates the worth of tomorrow's resources, must be rejected.

If we give ecological and population planning the attention and priority they deserve, we can reconcile the classic standard-of-consumption concept in our society with an environment-oriented index of living standards. New dimensions of conservation could then emerge in which a marriage of economics and ecology would occur.

Since the onset of the Industrial Revolution we have tormented ourselves by believing that the price we have to pay to enjoy the full benefits of mechanized industry is the blighting and befouling of the land and its renewable resources. This is false bookkeeping. It is rooted in the erroneous concept that to build a nation part of its permanent capital must be spent. We must dedicate ourselves to authentic conservation which maintains the productivity of our resource capital by wise use of resources and the maintenance of an environment that assures their continued full productivity. The more mature industrial revolution of tomorrow will find enlightened enterprise using our versatile technology within a framework that shows recognition of the fact that conservation is indispensable to the long-term wealth of nations.

The signs of this revolution are appearing in many places: the quest for clean energy by some segments of the electric-power industry; the aggressive if belated research by the petroleum and automotive industries for a clean combustion engine; the growing awareness in agriculture that fertilizers and pesticides that will leave nature unharmed must be produced; the realization by metal-using industries that recycling of "waste" metals is the only long-run solution to the problems of efficiency and self-sufficiency. All these, and other developments, are making conservation, for the first time, an accepted part of the business creed of this country. Were all entrepreneurs to be put on equal footing through the enactment of wise national laws that would establish performance standards, sound conservation practices would soon be part of the regular cost of doing business in America. Thereafter, the consumers of goods or services would pay for a cleaner technology, and, in return, get a much cleaner country.

Business initiative that anticipates and responds to legis-

102

lation must continue to underscore these new public pre-suppositions of private enterprise in this country:

We have the wealth and technical skill to make this a tidy, clean, well-ordered land without impairing our ability to harvest the fruits of a highly prosperous economic system.

Statesmanship must arrange an overdue marriage between the economics of production and the economics of beauty, and we must encourage the incentives and investments required to guarantee that no industrial activity degrades the over-all environment. To put it positively, our enterprise system must enhance living values by the design and location of its plants, by the control of its processes and effluents, and by the creation of a fulfilling milieu for its employees.

Prudence demands and history indicates the necessity of examining the nature and potential of new goods and services, so that we may understand their impact on man and nature before, not after, their use.

In the headlong rush to provide more and more consumer goods to supply what was assumed to be an ever-increasing population, we have forgotten, or perhaps never recognized, that we live on a finite planet whose environment is fragile, biologically interdependent, and self-contained. All the resources we require, except the energy of the sun, must be found on this earth and in its atmosphere. All of the wastes we produce by transforming these resources into evanescent products and services for consumers must be strewn or stored somewhere on the earth, unless they are recycled into the intricate system, which, but for the hand of man, is self-restoring. Nonrecycled wastes not only blight and befoul the environment, but also gradually diminish the irreplaceable resources of the system.

We have largely ignored the crucial importance of recycling materials. More seriously, we have ignored the vital fact that we are utterly dependent on the natural cycles of a thin and fragile layer of living plants and animals which exist where conditions of air, water, and solid earth combine to favor life, and which our scientists call the biosphere. These cycles can, of course, be seriously disrupted by our industrial and agricultural activities. Combustion in the furnaces and engines that power our industrial system produces such vast quantities of carbon dioxide that the foliage of the earth and the plankton of the sea may not be able to convert it back to carbon and oxygen. In turn, this may alter the heat-absorption capacity of the atmosphere and cause the earth's climate to grow warmer, melting the polar ice and raising the level of the seas. In addition to carbon and oxygen, there are numerous other elements that interact in this geochemistry—nitrogen, phosphorus, potassium, calcium, sulfur, and iron, for example—and that play indispensable roles in plant and animal metabolism.

Modern technology tends to disrupt these natural cycles by creating new materials—the aluminum can, the plastic container, and the proliferating synthetic goods—that are largely impervious to nature's way of dissolution and recomposition. The worst of these antinature materials, such as the "hard" synthetic detergents, not only overwhelm our sewage-disposal plants but also have long-term toxic effects on the ecological system itself.

We can invade and overpower the biosphere by dumping into it such large quantities of biologically active waste materials that the natural balance is simply swamped. This is most evident in the vicinity of urban complexes, where excessive quantities of sewage and other organic materials discharged into nearby waters disrupt whole biological communities. This has occurred in Lake Erie and at points in the Hudson River estuary, where these ersatz communities of organisms degrade the environment, and diminish the usefulness of resources or destroy them altogether.

Man also has the ability to create new toxic substances so virulent as to threaten the functioning of large sectors of the biosphere. The increasing abundance of manufactured pollutants can lead to ecological disasters. Until Rachel Carson's crusade against long-life pesticides aroused the nation, this problem was an abstruse concern of some scientists. Even the worry about nuclear wastes was confined, in the main, to scientific circles.

When one thinks in terms of centuries and millenniums, as all contemporary conservationists must, we should begin to worry about the ocean of oxygen in which we "swim" and realize that the burning of fossil fuels combined with long-term toxic effects of pesticides and other waste materials on plants could endanger the supply of the element that is literally the "breath of life." Wastes from synthetic agricultural fertilizers added to urban and industrial wastes might interfere with the nitrogen cycle and seriously disrupt the biosphere on a large scale. The potentially disastrous effects of pesticides, whose long-lasting poisons are broadcast everywhere on wind and tide, and then reconcentrated through food chains, are already verified. We are still haunted by the threat of a "silent spring."

These potential large-scale ecological disasters are well publicized. Less recognized, but equally important, is the danger of the slow undermining of natural balances, the insidious impoverishment of our environment through imbalances within communities of plants and animals.

Man, too, is part of this chain of life, linked inextricably with other, interacting, organisms. With his machines and technical prowess he is now an agent of change whose

105

cataclysmic powers dwarf the destructive but localized potential of nature's typhoons and earthquakes. Man is now the uneasy custodian of the Promethean flame. He can extinguish most forms of life on this planet and destroy the chain of life itself. He is no longer just another dancer in the system, but can control the terrible tempo of the dance itself and renew or destroy its essential rhythms.

The effects of man's destructive influence on his environment go beyond the physical impairments characterized by the broad terms "pollution" and "overconsumption." Too little professional attention has been given the effects of the environment on the human psyche. Until we become better able to measure the effects of human contact with the various components of the environment, we are almost forced to conclude that if we are not being subtly poisoned, unnerved, or irradiated, we have arrived at the good life.

A program that embraces the all-encompassing dimensions of the new conservation must be an integral part of Project 76. Our best efforts to bring population into balance and to build cities that will nourish the whole man cannot succeed unless, as a nation, we obey the imperatives of ecology. By accepting fully the discipline of this master science, the other branches of science will, in turn, become sensitive allies of beauty and order. Once we begin to work with, rather than against, the immanent laws of this planet, we will alter our national attitudes toward growth and devise the means of social control that will enable us to make sound stewardship our national policy.

The first century of our Industrial Revolution produced an incredible waste of resources and raw materials. Business had its trusts, but held nothing in trust for tomorrow. Resources we should have saved for other generations through recycling and sound husbandry were depleted.

Even today, the throwaway products in indestructible containers and the enormous solid wastes we spew across the landscape are reminders of the era of frontier abundance when we assumed we would never exhaust the richness or freshness of the land. The annual molting rite of the auto industry is another current example of egregious waste. The obsolescence of motor vehicles and the manufacture of thousands of poor-quality products that wear out overnight epitomize the conservation failures of American industry.

We must operate on a rigid recognition that the resources of this planet are finite. Exploitable concentrations of iron, copper, silver, and other basic minerals must be made to last as long as human life persists on earth. Common prudence demands that all metallic goods be constituted to retard obsolescence and to encourage recycling of "used-up" materials. Building automobiles so that their useful life is doubled (an easy feat for our automotive engineers) would constitute a huge saving in costly metals and irreplaceable materials. If this were done, the mineral base of the nation would be substantially enlarged. Even though prices had to be increased to pay for the superior design and improved workmanship, the total cost over the vehicle's longer life would be less, and the social benefits to both the consumer and the nation would be increased. Engineering that would facilitate easy recovery of metals for reuse would magnify our resources at little cost—indeed, at less than the present, unassessed social cost of large and small junk piles that mar the whole continent.

This will mean, of course, a drastic change in our approach to production. If, for example, we evaluate the impact of the aluminum can, the supersonic transport, or a new chemical pesticide before production, rather than after damage has occurred, safe and sane yardsticks of

107

progress will soon be established. We have acquired an astonishing capacity to make and sell almost anything, but we have blighted and contaminated the continent in the process. The old criterion of the national market place "Can it be made, mass produced, and sold at a profit?" is dangerously outdated. The task ahead is to win support for this more mature test: "Beyond its salability, will it work for man and with nature for the future?" We must learn to reckon profit by new accounting standards that do not discount the welfare of future generations.

The quality civilization we seek requires that we employ the wealth and skill we already possess—or can readily acquire—to redesign our technology and reorient our prowess so that we can pick the fruits of production without contaminating the tree of life. We can construct factories and plants that will assure industrial abundance without fouling our air, tainting our water, or despoiling the land. Should the rigors of this regimen mean that our future goods and services will cost a bit more to produce and to purchase, the consuming citizen will not fail to consider it a small price to pay for a clean country and a sanative future. For example, if wise laws make it mandatory that the price of a car include the extra cost required to render and recycle its carcass, the increase will be substantially offset by the resources thereby conserved. From now on, the fact that particular machines, goods, or services seem to be cheaper, more convenient, or a bit more efficient will not be decisive. The noise made, the effluvia expelled, the residues deposited, the unabsorbed wastes imposed on other generations must first be weighed in the balance.

The cost accounting of the upcoming age of ecology will encompass far more than the ordinary manufacturing and point-of-sale mentality. With a thought for the unborn, it will seek always to measure and maintain real wealth and to evaluate the tangible and intangible costs, the benefits and burdens foreseeable from any planned or proposed enterprise or activity. As we will soon learn, this will not inhibit, but, rather, pose a fresh challenge to, our capacities and our creativity. Put simply, this will entail an application of the systems approach (already accepted by advanced, computerized industries) to the intricate system of life itself. A new era is before us. It will challenge the leaders of business as never before to become conservation-minded, wealth-protecting guardians of the nation's environment. Unbridled growth, with its insistent emphasis on quantitative considerations, once fostered the short-run view among our men of business and even induced some spokesmen to glory in the ugliness and vulgarity of American life. But it is not likely we will hear again the blatant utterance a supposedly responsible advertising executive tossed off a few years ago: "Esthetes and apologists can rail at [the] vulgarity [of advertising], its brashness, its aggressiveness, its insistence, its lack of cultural values, its crass commercialism, its loudness and its singlemindedness—but let them rail. These are the qualities that have built the nation."

The emerging economics of beauty and the nascent economics of ecology are disciplines that will liberate man to pursue aims that value grace and joy, tidiness and tranquillity. Approval of such new dimensions and dynamics of conservation will not come easily. There will be resistance from some sectors of industry similar to the unenlightened outcry that greeted the first proposals a half-century ago that systematic compensation be paid to workmen for industrial injuries and that it be organized and "expensed" as part of the cost of doing business. I predict that this opposition will fail, for the quality-conscious men and women of the next generation will prefer machines that are quieter and safer, not faster; goods that can be produced and used with the least damage to the environment, and services that, while sacrificing no comfort or convenience, promote personal privacy and quiet.

The new dimensions of conservation will tend to give a more spacious outlook to men of labor and business, and accordingly make their institutions more discerning. These dimensions will also compel the architect, the industrial designer, and the government functionary to become practical environmentalists, aware of all the ramifications of change.

Only lack of will and intelligence can limit our performance, for whereas the cost of doing things right will be a wise investment in tomorrow, the cost of doing nothing will most assuredly be a calamity. There is no other alternative to the fight for a clean country and for an ecological regimen on this closed capsule earth, unless we elect to erect enclosed environments, become dome-dwelling denizens, and convert much of the hinterland into a vast dumping ground for our solid, gaseous, and liquid wastes.

To bring forth the new dimensions in conservation, specific implementing programs are essential. Such programs will translate spacious attitudes into specific actions, affecting life today and our legacy for tomorrow. Where land and water are concerned, it is excruciatingly clear to ecologists that much of the best preservation work already accomplished will be undone if we persist in the mismanagement of the biosphere. One day no birds will arrive at the wildlife refuges we have "saved," no butterflies will appear in the spring; fresh meadows, marshes, and ravines will be pre-empted as dumping grounds, and the repetitious sonic boom will shatter the peace of remote wilderness areas.

Traditional conservation must help bring nature and space into all sections of our cities. Among the "peaks" and "canyons" of the city, Sierra Clubs of tomorrow will fight to carve out hundreds of "canyon meadows" and mini-parks where plants and some wildlife can thrive, and children can play each day in fresh environs. A passion for urban amenities will cause these conservationists to hail a victory for new water-front promenades, lighted playgrounds, nature centers, mini-parks, or the restoration of a historic site or landmark building as an achievement as vital as the saving of a far-off wilderness. They will recognize that fine cities are inevitably garden cities, and argue the need for investments to preserve all nearby unspoiled lakes, marshes, rivers, and forests as common assets for the common good.

Beyond this, conventional conservation will enter the battle for the biosphere, and relate its assorted nature-saving plans and projects to a continuous search for an unimpaired environment. In the countryside its advocates will recognize the vital importance of access to riparian properties. Man is a water-loving animal, and we must move quickly to give him thousands of new "beachheads" to the oceans, lakes, and rivers of the land. Over the years, industry and men of wealth in search of private pleasure grounds have all but monopolized our shore lines. The power plants, the steel mills, the water-using industries have invariably sought to control the best riparian property. There is far too little public access today to the wonderland of water. Whether we purchase and "stockpile" riparian property, and develop it later, or buy enough land to make our shores readily reachable by all who want their solace, this is a "must" conservation project of the next two decades.

By the end of the next decade, local, state, and federal governments should sort out and acquire title and access to

111

those remaining sections of shore line suitable for state beach parks or national seashores. As part of this program, the Oregon Dunes and Michigan's Sleeping Bear Dunes should be added to the necklace of national sea and lakeshores already created by the Congress. Other spacious, unspoiled seashores now in our inventory of military lands, such as the long strands of Vandenberg Air Force Base, in California, and Matagorda Island, in Texas, should be given *conditional* national-seashore status now. The President should also propose an increase of the Land and Water Conservation Fund that would enable the federal government to pay seventy-five per cent of all acquisition costs of riparian properties acquired as recreation lands by the states or local governments.

A save-the-islands program is both necessary and practicable. These large and small water-captured nuggets of our landscape radiate the land mystique of our continent, for few have felt the heavy, contaminating hand of man. They will become harbors of refuge for man, and provide as much outdoor enjoyment as the most remote of inland islands of wilderness. The most precious of these island groups—the Apostle Islands of Lake Superior, Parramore Island in Virginia, most of the Golden Isles of Georgia, Smith Island in North Carolina, the Upper Biscayne Keys and the Ten Thousand Islands of Florida, the Gulf Islands of Florida, Alabama, and Mississippi, and Elizabeth Islands of Massachusetts—should be preserved as units of the national park system. The completion of the first U.S. island inventory gives the next President an opportunity to propose a fifteen-year program to turn most of our finest undeveloped islands into public treasures.

In 1872 the Congress passed a mining law which in its time seemed enlightened. Its purpose was to overcome the chaos in the developing West, for there was no code to adjust the disputes between conflicting miners seeking to develop the minerals of the public lands. In 1964, while enacting the Wilderness bill, Congress took a step backward by grafting into that law the concept that mineral exploration under this archaic act could continue in the wilderness until 1988. Nowhere on private lands in the United States does such a ludicrous policy persist as this law presents. For a mere $2.50 an acre for a lode claim or $5.00 an acre for a placer claim, a miner can secure through an association of claims several hundred acres of valuable public land or national forests worth hundreds of thousands of dollars for the minerals alone and tens of thousands of dollars for the timber. On the public estate mining is still like a search-and-destroy mission. The miner need not even be sure that he has a valuable mineral deposit. He may go onto the land and seize and disrupt it. Henceforth we must lease all minerals in our public estate in a way that will ensure their orderly development.

It should be our objective by 1980 to complete the establishment of our national wilderness system. At least five per cent of the U.S. land mass should ultimately be given permanent wilderness protection. Most of the acreage in the national wildlife refuges and at least two-thirds of the acreage in the national parks should be accorded wilderness status. Large tracts of the most primitive, unsullied public-domain lands in the West and in Alaska should also be given protection before development forecloses this final wilderness option.

The establishment of a National Scenic Rivers System could prove to be one of the notable pieces of conservation legislation of the 1960's. No later than 1985, the future of most of the major rivers of America should be decided. Future dams and reservoirs needed for flood control and power generation should be authorized only where these needs are urgent and meet the national-interest test. In order to give special protection to the finest fishing streams and to give the canoe, the kayak, and the raft a permanent place in the world of water, additional stretches of free-flowing rivers and tributaries with superior scenic and outdoor recreation values should be added to our national and state scenic-rivers system. The finest of our scenic rivers, such as the Potomac, the Buffalo in Arkansas, and the Upper Missouri in Montana, should carry the special designation of national rivers and should be managed by the National Park Service.

Beginning with Yellowstone in 1872, the United States pioneered the national park idea. Before the next decade ends we should perfect it by adding to our National Park System these natural masterpieces: a Voyageurs National Park in Minnesota, an Adirondack National Park in New York, a Kauai National Park in Hawaii, a Prairie National Park in Kansas, a Rainbow Bridge–Navajo National Park in Utah, a Sonoran Desert National Park in Arizona, and a Chitina Valley National Park in Alaska. The Congress should also convert such spacious national monuments as Glacier Bay and Katmai in Alaska, Death Valley in California, and an enlarged Capital Reef in Utah into true national parks. In addition, all privately owned "inholdings" in all national park areas should be purchased posthaste.

We should also add a new facet to our national parks preservation program: an urgent attention to those perhaps less scenic areas that are far more accessible to megalopolis. The Big Thicket, near Houston, is one example. Here, within a hundred-mile radius of three million people is a swamp-and-forest wilderness which abounds with rare flora and fauna. We should exploit all such opportunities for parks and wilderness near megalopolitan sprawls, particularly in the East, where few fine opportunities remain.

A new national system of trails should be supplemented by state and local trails, particularly walking and nature trails in urban areas, such as those in Seattle, Chicago, New York, and Phoenix. The initial national trails should include the Appalachian, Pacific Crest, Continental Divide, and Potomac Heritage trails. In due course, additional trails, such as the Long, North, Oregon, and Chisholm, may prove worthy additions. Jogging, cycling, bridle, and walking paths paralleling some of our scenic roads and parkways and skirting along our rivers and lakes should also be part of our national pattern of outdoor recreation.

If we do our work well, and capitalize on the insights science gives us into habitat maintenance, within a decade there should be no more endangered species of fish or wildlife. The main tasks of the friends of wild things, then, will be the enlargement of a hospitable habitat for the rare as well as the more common forms of wildlife, and the restoration of natural communities everywhere. To accomplish these ends the traditional wildlife-management concepts must be broadened to afford protection for more than merely the "target" species of the hunter and the angler. The interests of the urban dweller of tomorrow in enjoying the outdoor world demand that we develop ways to bring him into intimate contact with the natural world. State agencies must begin to reckon with a national population which is increasingly urban, proportionately less interested in fishing and hunting, and which with enlarged opportunities for education will become preoccupied with the more aesthetic aspects of nature.

Since the deterioration of the environment frequently takes place on private lands, local governments must encourage environmental protection by owners of rural property. All our educational efforts will fail if owners of private land cannot be persuaded to practice conservation. Hunting and fishing cannot survive without a viable habitat for wildlife. Once we rightly regard wildlife as a product of the land—with a market value based on the recreation wildlife resources can supply—we can provide the incentive private landowners must have if wildlife conservation is to make its maximum contribution to the nation's future.

Heeding Thoreau's advice, all communities should consider themselves poor unless they own and administer with care at least one expansive, close-by marsh, forest, or nature laboratory of sufficient size to be a classroom for the young and an outdoor museum for all. This idea is already catching on. When the citizens of northern New Jersey rejected a jet airport, with its highly advertised thirty thousand jobs, and raised over a million dollars to save the Great Swamp as a regional nature sanctuary, the living values for miles around were enhanced. Even a community as small as Danville, Kentucky (population twelve thousand five hundred), has found that a recently acquired five hundred-acre woodland wildlife refuge is an asset to the entire community.

The coastal zone, where fresh and salt waters intermingle with the conflicting forces of current and winds and tides, is a zone of conflicting human interests. The resources of estuaries, bays, shore lines, and continental shelf have been fought over, abused by navigation, manufacturing, and recreation interests for years, with nature and recreation usually on the losing side of the argument. Some of our estuaries have an amazing level of fertility, exceeding many times that of even the best agricultural land. Estuaries are the nursing grounds for seventy per cent of the fish commercially caught in the United States and its coastal waters. Through the estuaries swim salmon, shad, and other anadromous fish. The fertility of the estuaries also attracts water birds, and many of our most important migratory species spend a portion of their lives in estuaries: the various kinds of ducks, the herons, and the whooping cranes. The estuaries also represent a unique area for recreation, a place where human values can be restored by the quiet and solitude of fishing in the mangrove swamps of Florida or in the marshes of Georgia or in the fjords of the Northwest.

But most of our major cities are located on estuaries also, and their increase in population places an ever increasing demand on the estuaries for all kinds of industrial and commercial purposes. The simple truth is that the size of the human population is really the key to the ultimate control of the quality of the environment. In the meantime, the struggle over the estuaries reaches its highest pitch between those who would dredge and fill, dump the waste products of the cities, pollute with oil and toxic chemicals, and those who want to preserve the estuaries in their natural state for recreation and for their scenic value, for fishing and for supplies of drinking water.

We must aggressively enlarge our coastal wildlife refuges, expand our national seashores wherever possible, and encourage the states to acquire and protect all of the coastal marine lands needed to save these offshore cradles of the sea. Pollution must be checked, physical destruction brought under control, and creative imagination used to enlarge the possibilities for public enjoyment of coral reefs, giant kelp beds, and the fascination of the underwater world. We need legislation to manage estuaries in such a way as to preserve their values while at the same time using them as important avenues of commerce and industry. The key to this coexistence of conflicting uses

117

is, of course, clean water. If we can maintain unpolluted waters in the estuaries, then many of these competing uses will in fact be able to live alongside each other, and our national utilization will be greatly enhanced.

It should become a matter of national policy that no estuary be filled or marsh drained unless it serves an overriding national interest. We can no longer treat marshes as wastelands to be filled in for real-estate development. The estuarine zone is too valuable to the ecology of our marine life and for the social needs of our citizens.

Three further steps are necessary to round out the work of conventional conservation: vigorous laws requiring the reclamation of surface-mined land should be enacted, local ordinances should require natural screening of the innumerable dumps and eyesores that mar our cityscapes and countrysides, and all states should follow Vermont's lead and prohibit billboards in the countryside in favor of well-planned sign plazas and public-information programs to enlighten the traveler.

We have failed for too long to give balance to our highway system. The time has come to add new humanizing elements to its planning. We should widen right of ways so that the roadways of tomorrow will become corridors of safe travel featuring protected walkways and bridle and bicycle paths interlaced with abutting natural lands which add to our total estate for outdoor recreation. We should also build a nationwide system of scenic parkways patterned after the superb Blue Ridge Parkway, which winds along the eastern edge of the Appalachian Mountains from northern Virginia to the Great Smoky Mountains. Other scenic parkways worthy of early consideration would be a Great River Road bisecting the Mississippi heartland, an Allegheny Parkway in West Virginia, Virginia, Kentucky, and Maryland, and a Lewis and Clark Trail Parkway paralleling the route of great explorers. When the current interstate highway program is completed in the early 1970's, a national system of scenic highways should be given a high priority in the new program, and be financed entirely from the Highway Trust Fund.

The remaining public-domain lands belonging to the nation should be classified for retention as part of the permanent national estate and designated as "national resource lands." Moreover, they should be put under multiple-use management, with particular attention to their outdoor-recreation potential.

A conservation program of this magnitude should not be suggested without a parallel recommendation for funding. The Land and Water Conservation Fund, established by the Congress in 1964, should be enlarged as required to carry out these objectives, with adequate funds earmarked from the revenues derived from exploitation of the re- sources of the continental shelf. Through this device, the nation would insure that the income from capital assets owned by the people—the depletable mineral wealth of our continental shelf—is reinvested in highest-quality scenic, wildlife, and outdoor recreation areas which will be owned by the American people in perpetuity.

If it is to be ultimately successful, the new conservation must be global. We are but a small fraction of the human population on the earth. We cannot hope to create an oasis of cleanliness or tranquillity or balance in the midst of an ill-managed world. There will be no isolated nations in the world of tomorrow. The biosphere is a common possession, and must be managed by a common international hus- bandry that respects its inner laws. Where nature is con- cerned, the earth is now too shrunken to wall out other nations. The Nuclear Test Ban Treaty of 1963 was far more than a diplomatic triumph of the Cold War; it was a conservation-of-life treaty of the first magnitude.

We must bring the human population of this planet

119

into balance with its resources, and learn to avoid fouling our environment so that we make possible for men everywhere not mere animalistic survival but a life that permits the enjoyment of basic human values, the beauties of nature and of art, the flowering of individual creativity. Our traumatic technology can now control enormous sources of energy and employ techniques that can affect even some of the global cycles of chemistry and biology. The poisoning of the oceans and of the atmosphere and the disruption of the oxygen and nitrogen cycles could be lethal for man everywhere. Our technology is now pervasive enough to produce changes in world climate, even as inadvertent side effects, which could melt enough of the world's glaciers to cause the inundation of all coastal cities. Caution compels us to recognize that a sensitive, well-planned program of international stewardship of the resources of air and water is now essential and must soon lead to new patterns of global co-operation.

To ensure an effective national focus for action, several members of Congress have already proposed the creation of a Council of Environmental Advisers to balance and complement the work of the Council of Economic Advisers. This council would help the President, the Congress, and the country evaluate all plans for national development to the end that governmental decisions would enhance the environment and give full effect to the new dimensions of conservation. The Department of the Interior should be redesignated the nation's Department of Natural Resources and Environment and be given the mission of full responsibility for conservation.

At long last, let us learn to be skeptical of our prowess and sensitive in judging all proposals for growth and change. Restraint should be the watchword, for less *will* be more as we improve our skills in making policies for the

120

improvement of population and environment. We have already learned—or should have by now—that posterity will honor us more for the roads and dams we do not build in areas having irreplaceable scenic and recreational values than for those we do. These new insights should cause us to slacken, and ultimately cease, the constant subtraction from our common estate. Beauty and order should frame everyday life. The poet craves them, religion celebrates them, the democratic philosophy assumes them, and the latent naturalist and artist in every man thrives in their presence. The essence of the new conservation, then, will reside in the vision and diligence we bring to our deepening sense of stewardship over the real capital of the nation.

7. Population, Parenthood, and the Quality of Life

"Of all valuable things on earth, man is most valuable because he is an end, not a means. The revolution today is for him, that his dignity might at long last be realized on earth, as well as in heaven. No matter what his race, his color, his country, his culture, or his religion or the lack of it, he is a res *sacra, a sacred thing, a person who deserves better of this world if his inner dignity is not to be lost in the outer indignity of so much that is utterly inhuman in modern life."* —THEODORE M. HESBURGH

"The balanced economy we must now seek will place its emphasis not on the horsepower it consumes but on the manpower it releases: it will translate energy into leisure and leisure into life." —LEWIS MUMFORD

Dr. Donald Bogue's thoughtful contradiction, explored in Chapter Three, of the estimate so slavishly accepted by most public officials—that by the end of this century our population will reach three hundred million—may prove to be a decisive development in our history. His demographic studies cause him to reject the more conventional calculations and conclude that a decelerated population swing has already begun in the 1960's, a trend that should actually level off the population at about two hundred and twenty million within the next decade. It is difficult to know if he is right or wrong. Predictions and projections, as all marketing experts and budget-makers know, are

122

interpretations which, though based on facts, assume continuing momentum to turn them into truths. As such, they can be instruments of persuasion or psychological facts, and thus have a way of turning into self-fulfilling prophecies.

In considering Dr. Bogue's demographic projection, therefore, the element of the psychological fact should be included and underscored. Restraint in this case *is* action. Less—if we accept it—*is* more. We are not, after all, frogs in a spring pond, but a people with a house that, no matter how spacious we think it, remains finite. It will be hard, at first, to adjust our thinking to the realities inherent in a new gospel of rational growth, but our future demands that we now make the effort.

The trend toward a stable population that Dr. Bogue has described is not a response to an official national population policy, for there is none. It is, rather, the sum of myriad individual decisions men and women have made about their future. The slowing pace would be measurably slower if more of the births counted in Dr. Bogue's studies had been planned births. Most probably were not. What is significant, however, is that restraint and control, not accident, is now a considerable factor and must remain so. Those exercising restraint have reached, in effect, decisions based in varying degrees on their faith in or fears of the future, and their estimate of their own and society's capacity to sustain their children at an enriched and enriching opportunity level. Dr. Bogue's prediction, and the trend he has underscored, should encourage us to investigate all the reasons involved. What we discover will help us to formulate a rational population policy expressing just what we want for the future.

Among the influences that have slowed our human growth rate are these: the contraceptive pill and the easy

123

availability of modern family-planning techniques (controls that may soon appear "primitive" when new medical devices, less intrusive, perhaps, in the physiological processes, come into use) ; the antihuman aspects of urban existence in twentieth-century America; a realization that opportunities open to children increase as the capacity of parents increases to invest in those educational and extraeducational experiences and activities that nurture young minds; a growing awareness of the importance of a modicum of serenity and useful leisure time, and of the difficulties in finding either in a congested, pressure-cooker environment; the uncertainties of a turbulent world, where war is not the only threat, but in which family planning— the *real* life insurance—is perhaps the only ultimate road to peace and to a wide range of options for each individual, and the realization that "good" parents should have only those children whose full development they are prepared to nurture, and that in the home, as well as in society, children of quality are preferable to quantities of children.

If Dr. Bogue is correct—an outcome devoutly to be wished—the end of the population explosion in the United States is in sight. There is a difference, however, between goals visible and goals achieved. To assure the population level Dr. Bogue foresees, public as well as private action will have to be taken. Yet, before we make any public decision, we must make a study of what our optimum population should be.

We need a Population Policy Commission of eminent and expert Americans empowered to identify the determinants and direction of new "growth." Perhaps more important than the optimum such a commission would suggest will be the methods and norms it adopts to reach its recommendations. It is time our population-distribution patterns were studied, in order that the optimum finally suggested accurately reflect the cultural, agricultural, commercial, climatic, and other characteristics peculiar to each region of the country. Each will likely suggest that deriving from our stabilized regional populations are new options available to individuals, city planners, design teams, businessmen, and government. Relieved of the pressure of dealing constantly with the accommodation of an excessive annual population increment, all could devote their capacities and creativity to achieving environmental excellence, to the greater humanization of man, and to those long-ignored but increasingly vital relationships and distribution patterns that the leveling off of our human growth curve—for the first time—will make possible.

By 1976, sensible supporting programs could be well underway that would, in fact, become a new blueprint for national growth based on qualitative human betterment, rather than on mere numbers of people or the gross national product. This new blueprint would, of course, give strong impetus to family planning, to a serious effort at sex education in the schools, and to the wide dissemination of birth-control information and devices. It might also require that we reconsider and revise our tax policies in relation to their encouragement of large families. Once we agree on an optimum population for our nation, prospectively our tax incentives or exemptions should aid the achievement of the national purpose. It ought to be in line with our current analysis of the various guaranteed annual-income and negative-income-tax proposals.

Much more than the wider and wiser use of birth control and family planning is implied in the stabilizing of our population. It would also manifest a will, and an opportunity, to enlarge the margins of life by a more constructive approach to marriage and new attitudes toward parenthood. We must talk less about the unlimited right

125

of married couples to have children, and more about the basic birthright of every child to enjoy parental love and care that is as much family-centered as it is child-centered, that is life-promoting rather than a sedulous preparation for material success.

We might begin by recognizing that a significant number of the adults in this country—perhaps a larger percentage than we care to admit—are poorly qualified by temperament or inherent personal traits to rear children. It takes more than physical capacity to make a parent and far more than mere means to make an effective one. Some persons are not temperamentally fit for marriage; others, though married, should not have children. This is not something to be regulated by law, but should evolve out of a change of attitude toward the conventional concept of marriage. All lives are not enhanced by marital union; parenthood is not necessarily a fulfillment for every married couple. Let us ease the social stigma of singlehood, and encourage, even by our tax laws, those who are inclined to direct their talents elsewhere. Let us cease our thoughtless disapproval of childless marriages and lend moral support to those who perhaps rightly shun the complex and demanding task of child nurture. We must recognize that the talent for child care is a gift not all possess, and abandon our disapproval of those who feel parenthood would frustrate rather than fulfill. Among the most tragic unpunishable "crimes" in the world today is the permanent injury done young bodies and minds by the demoralizing and inhuman acts of mental and physical brutality committed against children by totally unfit parents.

Another factor to be considered is the high divorce rate among the young. This should be a powerful argument for late marriage. It is folly to marry before one has had a full opportunity to assess the joys and burdens of the modern world. There is nothing in biology or common sense that is offended by the notion that marriage for young women should be avoided before, say, twenty-three, and for young men before twenty-five or thirty. Experience tells us there are no magic numbers, that restraint is usually the course of wisdom. Superior nutrition means physical maturity comes earlier, yet mental and moral maturity, based as they are on accumulated experience, come later. Prolonged higher education for much larger numbers of people, by extending the training period, means not much more than subsistence income while it goes on, and so does not produce a situation in which marriage can flourish without hazard. Fostering late marriage would not only reduce our divorce rate and minimize the number of broken homes, but also serve as a reminder to the young that self-knowledge, which brings discernment of limitations and strengths, deepens with experience and makes possible sound decisions about life and parenthood. Late marriage, in a society where the life expectancy has greatly increased, does not necessarily mean less marriage. Quality is what counts, and fewer years of marriage may mean years far richer.

Society should encourage, on the other hand, those who have the capacity to be successful parents. Increasingly, the design of our cities and American work patterns have eliminated the father from the family scene. In the nineteenth century, the family farm and the equine scale in both city and country kept nearly everyone in sight and call of each other all day long. This, of course, deepened the contact between children and parents. But this contact between the generations has now disappeared for the majority of Americans. The economics of commercial farming have rendered the family far less viable with the passing of each year; and as industrialization has quickened urbanization the old intimacy of daily work and living patterns has largely disappeared; a new pattern of life for most Americans in this largely middle-class nation has been created. Today, the phenomena of the commuting father and the working mother often occur in the same family. This usually means that both parents see their children only briefly at the beginning and end of each workday. The children are thus brought up by people outside the family. And in those families where the mother does remain at home, the daily parental responsibility is wholly hers. It is she who must cope, not only with the routine chores of cooking, homework, and bedtime, but also with more than her share of handling the crucial duties of discipline and child guidance. "Coping" is hardly what parenthood should mean. Regardless of her efficiency as a homemaker and regardless of her loving capacity as a mother, this is not the ideal we should strive for. The nature of the life pattern within which the mother and father live defines their opportunities as parents.

Not the least encouragement to be derived from Dr. Bogue's projection is that we no longer must accept the inevitability of these defining patterns. A planned population will make possible the shaping of them by rational choice and end our blind acceptance of obsolete norms of reproduction and work.

For instance, in a slow-growth society in which each family may choose its optimum size, the two-child family should become the norm. Once this occurs we can begin to tap our richest reservoir of unused talent—the creative capacities of women. Once we no longer overwhelm ourselves with child rearing, but restore it to its proper qualitative primacy, women will be free, at the appropriate time, to make other singular contributions to society in all fields of human endeavor. By our third century, child rearing, without losing its supreme importance, will be matched more closely to the rational fulfillment of women. Double options will exist for those who elect both motherhood and careers—and without threat to either's completion. The real emancipation of women will have arrived when *both* sexes are deeply involved in the vital work of their communities. Today, despite all the advances in education, it is still unusual for women to *want* jobs in certain fields. Even where overt barriers to careers no longer exist, stultifying forces are at work that cause too many women to restrict their own aspirations and perspectives.

A stabilized population will also have a beneficient effect on our educational system. Once educators can turn their undivided attention to the individual and to quality instruction, the performance of the educational system will improve all along the line. The student unrest characteristic of the late 1960's is a phenomenon that no doubt says much about student dissatisfaction with the military draft and the society that requires it. But it also says quite as much about the neglect of personal relationships at some of our large impersonal institutions. It was not mere coincidence, for example, that the University of California's campus at Berkeley began to erupt about the same time that President Clark Kerr's volume explaining the virtues of the "multiversity" appeared in print.

As long as many university officials are required to employ most of their executive energy as the politicians and promoters of "growth," we can anticipate that students will feel they are being more processed than educated. But once the expansion scramble slows, school administrators will be able to turn to the search for excellence and give primacy to persons. Once academic executives are free to concentrate on innovation in curricula, the upgrading of faculties, and the democratization of the collegiate community, student, not campus, growth will become their preoccupation.

We should make a determined effort—and this will mean elevating salaries and levying taxes to meet them—to recruit more males for the faculties of our elementary and middle schools. Far too many of our elementary-school staffs, and to a lesser extent our junior-high and high-school staffs, are preponderantly female. This corrective action would bring our children's early school years into a truer balance with the rest of life.

We should also support the renaissance currently going on in much teacher preparation, and urge the expansion of those experimental programs aimed toward bringing parents into the daily routine of the elementary school. The exceedingly valuable, though seriously underfunded, pre-school Head Start programs across the nation open important opportunities for such steady and constructive contact between school and community. We should devise similar programs to ease the transitions between education and the practical workaday world.

Good educators accept the validity of Ralph Waldo Emerson's remark that "The true test of a civilization is not the census, nor the size of cities, nor the crops . . . but the kind of man the country turns out." It defines the real challenge to education today.

Population equilibrium would also speed up the much discussed and much misunderstood "leisure revolution." A shortened workweek and rapidly developing technologies forecast for tomorrow a larger margin of leisure for all citizens. The problem up to now has been the unequal distribution of leisure through the range of occupations, but as the two-week vacation increases to a month and occupations themselves become more humane, parents and children and others will have new opportunities to turn leisure time to personal advantage. Self-culture will deepen, and we will be less likely to succumb to the seductions of sedentary spectatorship, travel for which we are unready, and all the consuming pursuits of misguided affluence.

We have consistently underrated the contribution of sports to our society. Games and playing fields require an all-men-are-equal ethic. They have brought us closer to ideal democracy than perhaps any other activity we embrace as a people. It is not enough today to be concerned only with the expansion of our parks, any more than it is sufficient for us to be satisfied with the commercial successes of intercollegiate and professional athletics. We must give games back to the people wherever possible, to aid their physical and emotional development. We should expand intramural athletic programs within all of our schools, broaden our neighborhood recreation programs for all family members, give the Little Leagues back to the children, and, by democratizing its base, help return the Olympics to the spirit with which they were imbued at the time of their origination. The ancient Greeks were right—good games involve more than mere exercise.

The more deliberate pace of life in an America with a stabilized population will provide not only the time for reflection and growth with distinction, but also may well teach us to cultivate the gentler sides of our natures, to awaken to the arts and to sense the lasting satisfactions of altruism. The retired business executive contributing his skills in helping an underdeveloped nation start a new industry (through the voluntary Executive Corps formed by New York business leaders) is living a far more meaningful life than his superannuated colleague golfing the winter away in Florida. Retired workers and teachers who volunteer to help their cities alleviate the consequences of social decay will be ten times more satisfied than those who flit impatiently from one vacuous hobby to another. "Involvement" and "participation" are sure to be key concepts in the richer community life of tomorrow. One of the most fulfilled persons I have ever met is the retired California coach who came to Washington and became a successful one-man "lobby" for civil-rights legislation. Budd Schulberg, the novelist and Hollywood writer who spends his spare time running creative-writing clinics in the ghettos, has shown how one individual can help young people whose gifts have been wholly overlooked find themselves.

The end we should seek is individual development made possible by newly opened doors of formal and informal adult education. A particularly heavy burden will rest in future years on labor unions and local governments to enlarge the horizons of workers drained by drudgery. The self-renewal of which John W. Gardner has written with such persuasion and insight is, of course, the key to a leisure that leads to education, not vegetation. Education and leisure are linked, for education is more than preparation for given kinds of work. Its essence is the use of leisure in a continuous self-culture that deepens personal growth and leads to the adventures that only an active mind can undertake.

If we will permit ourselves to use both our wealth and our wisdom, we can develop high potentials for the enhancement of the family by the careful creation of rebuilt environments and new towns, both within and without our present urban complexes. The typical suburban development of the postwar era provided housing, and gave buyers the satisfaction of owning a small tract of land, but usually did not create real communities. In this it failed where it needed most to succeed. Most of what it touched—the natural loveliness and spaciousness that characterized, for example, the Los Angeles and Long Island environments of the 1920's—was altered beyond recognition. What is needed is not the hurried construction of post-and-beam look-alike houses in citrus groves or potato fields, but a disposition to give reasonable reign to the regional planner's sense of ecological balance. The key questions should have been:

How should a new town site be selected?

How many people should it have?

How many levels of employment, given its locale, can be planned for it?

How can it be made to be more than just another white, middle-class bedroom suburb?

How can we ensure the economic viability of the alternatives?

There is some landmark twentieth-century American experience to consult. Radburn, in New Jersey, a private project planned in 1929, and Greenbelt, in Maryland, a project encouraged by the U.S. Resettlement Administration in the mid-1930's, were isolated achievements in human-scale urbanization. However, a good new-town plan should be a master amenity from which other amenities flow. By assuming, as the law of its development, that the human scale is the measure of the public interest, it should provide a practical balance between land, population density, work, rest, and play. In the simplest terms, its aim should be to provide a setting that makes possible a humane pattern of living for all its inhabitants.

Reston, a new town in the Virginia suburbs of Washington, is a striking contemporary example. Its seven-year history has seen a cycle of critical acclaim and economic frustration resulting largely from the high-minded and single-minded purpose of its founder, Robert E. Simon, Jr., to provide a humane setting for human living. From the beginning. the design criteria spelled out a form that would provide a balanced and intermingled internal environment: work/play, urban/natural, cultural/commercial. One of the earliest controversies surrounded Simon's intention to provide a unified diversity of residences, offices, and shops in a central plaza area, which—until an exception was granted—violated the conventional wisdom of local zoning. In contrast to the plans of his peer James Rouse, whose somewhat similar project is underway in nearby Columbia, Maryland, Simon expressed his community concept in this way: "Our town center will look more like an urban center. . . . The town center of Columbia isn't restricted to stores, but the stores are in one area, the office buildings in another, and the recreation in another. I think it is pleasanter and more efficient to have the uses intermingled so that you have apartments—high rise and low rise—townhouses, stores, museum, concert hall, restaurants all mixed together the way it would be in a wonderful city." This approach most definitely expands the "whole-life" experience of the residents, as do other design aspects of this new town. Except for the locating of Reston in a typical subdivision area, conventional development was not followed. Living units are clustered closely together. They are separated from other clusters by a continuous skeletal structure of natural open space. Even though the density is greater than that of most subdivisions, the appearance, and experience, is one of intimate relationship to the out-of-doors and an urban juxtaposition that represents a happy blend of the best medieval and the best modern design. Separated from the road network there is a path system for walkers and cyclists that makes such activity an attraction instead of a hazard. The plan

134

adds new dimensions to the lives of the residents. In the late summer evenings, fathers and sons can be seen fishing together or flying a kite a short walk from their homes. Families stroll downtown in a manner reminiscent of the nostalgic small-town Saturday night of yesteryear. Others sit on terraces or balconies reading and conversing. The only audible sounds are usually the breeze in the trees and the laughter of children.

Reston, however, is to be seen only as an example of the potential—not the fulfillment—of design to shape the social experience. Its financial troubles have been blamed on the nonmarketability of these new design concepts; in reality, the financial problems have their basis in the same failures that prevent the residents from enjoying to the fullest the very amenities that first attracted them. Reston has two built-in flaws: lack of local economic activity to provide employment in Reston, and the absence of rapid transit to Washington. A two-hour round trip makes it almost impossible to develop the enriching extra elements of a catholic culture; and low-income families cannot afford the extra cost of commuting by car. Until indigenous economic activity develops, the diversity envisioned by Simon is ruled out.

But its inability to overcome its circumstances should not obscure the central lesson of Reston: town planning can profoundly affect our lives. In countering charges that it is overplanned, it is ironic that its developers have stated that they planned "land, not lives." This is only superficially true. The whole thrust and significance of their enterprise demonstrates that in fact the two are unalterably intertwined. The effect of land on lives is impossible to overestimate.

A crucial measure of the success of a plan for a new or an old town—the degree to which it becomes a master amenity

—is the extent to which it enlarges the opportunities for parenthood and enables family life to flourish. This is not to suggest a return to the pastoral, farm-family pattern of nineteenth-century living, but a rearrangement of our physical environment could help resolve many of our social dilemmas. And the converse is equally true. Our design failures have contributed, more than we realize, to the quiet despair, confusion, and alienation that result in divorce, delinquency, and unhappiness.

In a slow-growth society, parenthood will become an even more important calling of the next generation, a personal accomplishment with enormous public consequences. Those parents who have the patience and whose pattern of living gives them the time to bring out the joy and whet the creative curiosity of the young will be prized citizens of our democracy. We prate far too much about the "failure of society" when misreared children become antisocial adults. This sentimental indulgence in social guilt tends to evaporate when it becomes clear that many social ills and violent antisocial acts are traceable to the pathetic failure of unqualified nonparents, rich, middle class, and poor, who mentally and physically maim their own unwanted offspring.

A much higher concept of parental responsibility will make us demand more of the cities of the future. The parents of tomorrow will consider a city environment intolerable if it does not provide every child the living rights of abundant nearby places to play, a green sheath of trees and shrubs to bring some wildlife near every window, free access to an outdoor recreation program that includes the full range of sports, and a ready relationship to the visual and performing arts. Those American communities of the year 2000 that deny their young the simple and safe opportunity to fly a kite, ride a bike, boat and swim in a river or pond, keep a pet, or come to know the arts will be the run-down Appalachias and the disordered Detroits of our twenty-first century.

The potency of design to influence quality living goes far beyond the planning of the physical arrangements of cities. In its highest and best sense, design is the art of bringing order and balance out of seemingly unrelated elements. Its principles apply as well to the structuring of our organizations and institutions.

We need to reconsider the belief that the whole spectrum of our life patterns is inevitable. Nothing in society is inevitable any longer. The remaining years of this century hold out almost unlimited possibilities. All decisions affecting our future should reflect imagination and a full realization of human potentials. For each effect there is a cause; for each identifiable defect there is a specific remedy. This is the hope of both the new towns in town and the new towns in the countryside, and the real promise of superior design. For too long our cities, our land, and our institutions have diminished our lives. It is now within our power, and within the capacity of our wealth and technical skill, to permit our aspirations to shape our environment—and our lives.

Population stability offers many opportunities, but none will be greater than the chance to build great cities and to bring our man-land equation into balance. The development of a rational population policy for the nation could be the finest legacy of our generation. To the people on other crowded continents it will offer hope. For us it will mean a precious opportunity to achieve an ecological equilibrium on this continent, to bring the works of man and nature into harmony, and to guarantee that future generations will live in a land of promise.

8. The Renewal of Politics

*"In short, men must be discriminating appraisers of
their society, knowing coolly and precisely what it is
about society that thwarts or limits them and therefore needs modification. And so must they be discriminating protectors of their institutions, preserving
those features that nourish and strengthen them and
make them more free. To fit themselves for such tasks,
they must be sufficiently serious to study their institutions; sufficiently dedicated to become expert in the
art of modifying them."* —JOHN W. GARDNER

Project 76 and the complementary plans and programs
outlined in this book hold the promise of resolving our
internal crisis and raising the quality of life in this country, but they demand an innovative approach to politics
and a willingness to modernize our essential institutions of
government. If we are to rebuild our cities on a noble scale
and make the early decades of our third century an unprecedented period of social progress, we must develop a
fresh framework for political action, make a historic shift
of power and responsibility to local governments, and
develop a politics of participation that will enlist the
energy and good will of most of our citizens.

The transforming work of a Project 76 will require that we drink once more from the fountain of 1776, and view the American prospect with the same social energy, optimism, and creative thought that attended the founding of this nation.

The wartime and peacetime crises of this century have exerted a centripetal pull that has made Washington the main action center of our politics. Since the Wilson Administration, but notably since the New Deal days, this fact has provoked a sterile argument about the merits of national versus state leadership. The imperious issues that confront us now, however, are in the cities where nearly three-fourths of our people reside, and we should therefore adapt our representative political institutions and practices to meet this obvious reality.

A crisis of efficiency and a crisis of democracy have come together in the cities. The next generation confronts a challenge whose dimensions are unexampled in our history. We can respond indifferently to it (amid calls for more police, and more "roof-repair" remedies by desperate local governments whose resources are consumed by the imperatives of day-to-day responsibilities) or by fresh efforts to overhaul and rejuvenate all levels of government. The important role of legislative reapportionment under the Supreme Court's one-man-one-vote principle has already enlivened and liberalized our politics.

If one cure for the sickness of the cities is for the states to assume nearly full financing of the operating costs of public education (as Delaware and New Mexico already have done), and for the federal government to provide liberal "even-break" funds for disadvantaged children (as it has already done to a limited extent under the Elementary and Secondary Education Act of 1965), then we should quickly alter the patterns of school finance. If welfare costs should be a national responsibility (as they are today in nearly all modern nations), then Washington should relieve the local governments of this burden (by a well-conceived system of income supplements designed to encourage self-sufficiency) and permit local funds and energies to be used on other vital programs of social betterment. Our problem has not been that the cities do not know what is wrong. For years most mayors have been underscoring the causes and proposing the cures for the predicaments of their cities. As long as the federal and state governments command the superior sources of tax revenues, the cities will lack the wherewithal to do more than provide minimum public services.

Obsolete state laws and constitutions are another cause of the inadequacy of local governments. One of the most discouraging developments of the last year has been the rejection of improved new constitutions—Maryland is an example—by the electorate. This form of ostrichism can be defeated only by broadening the base of representation to state constitutional conventions and by determined statewide campaigns to generate support for constitutional reform. By rationing power and restricting prerogatives prejudicially, the many states have put a strangle hold on their cities. It is a disgrace that mayors must go as beggars to statehouses, or live in the hope that some Washington "grant" will bail them out of the next crisis. This condition of affairs symbolizes not so much a "failure" of municipal government as a failure of state and federal leadership to respond to the growing crises of urban America.

The states must begin now to remove restrictions on the debt-carrying and taxing capacities of local governments, to change constitutional and charter criteria to make possible the annexation of adjacent areas and mini-cities, and, by enlarging and adding new local zoning powers, to make

140

building and housing codes vehicles of action, not obstruction. We will find it impossible to revitalize local governments unless the states confer on them problem-solving power, and unless both federal and state governments create conditions of financial solvency that will make large-scale action possible. Unless they do, our city fathers will continue to be tied to stopgap programs and one-summer-at-a-time holding operations. The mayors who walk the summer streets of our cities can only hope to buy time until other governments act and produce programs that can change the lives and living standards of their people. The underlying causes of ghetto despair and unrest cannot be met by displays of personal concern and courage on the sidewalk. The mayors and their people share a mutual powerlessness, and it is this shared weakness that must be remedied.

An urgent need in the heavily populated states is for regional entities of government that can imaginatively and effectively deal with problems that sprawl over arbitrary state and municipal boundaries. We must have interstate river-basin commissions (modeled on the Delaware River Basin Commission, with the federal government as a partner) to manage the water future of regions that share the same river. The striking success of such regional institutions as the Metropolitan Water District of Southern California (the largest wholesaler of fresh water in the world) should have told us several decades ago that vast public-works projects can be carried out at the regional level only if the power and responsibility required to get results are conferred.

The states must also create commuter-transportation authorities to make rapid mass transit a reality in congested metropolitan regions. San Francisco's Bay Area Rapid Transit Authority is a good model. Governor

141

Nelson Rockefeller's Metropolitan Commuter Transportation Authority (given vast power through a statewide referendum in 1968 to expand the New York subway system, overhaul tri-state commuter transportation, and provide easy rapid transit to airports) represents the total approach to mass transportation that deserves imitation by the populous states.

Innovation by the states, to be sure, must not be confined to regional problems alone. State leadership must help tackle local problems from the broader statewide perspective. New Jersey's Governor Richard J. Hughes recently proposed what is probably the first comprehensive state program directed toward the urban crisis. Of particular significance was his concurrent advocacy of an income tax which would provide the state with the means—initially, one hundred and twenty-six million dollars—to attack decay and provide first-rate public services. This attempt to meet social responsibilities with a graduated income tax is not, in itself, a revolutionary concept. But, even though it was defeated by a myopic legislature, it continues to be a bold example of independent initiative to those politicians who would rather await largesse from Washington than rely on their own untapped tax resources. And New York's Governor Rockefeller has proposed a revolutionary Urban Development Corporation that is also noteworthy. This superagency would have sweeping authority to condemn property, to ignore, if necessary, local building and zoning codes, and could offer special incentives to venture capital to renovate whole sections of cities. This proposal holds promise, but Michael Harrington has expressed concern that its weak guidelines could "repeat the Title I scandals, the failures of urban renewal . . . in New York," and Mayor Lindsay has expressed reservations about its invasion of home-rule pre-

142

rogatives. These are correctable details, however. The important thing these two examples show is that some governors are at last proposing bold plans for large-scale renovation of cities. This is shown, too, in Governor Rockefeller's water-pollution, rapid-transit, and urban-redevelopment legislation, which has set the stage for a concerted campaign to tackle problems that were considered "insoluble" a few years ago.

New agencies of this kind will add a professional-management dimension to the urban scene. The pragmatic, problem-solving experts who must formulate and execute new patterns of federal-state-local partnerships should be forerunners of a new political leadership, which will always carry its case to the people.

Once we undertake something as bold as Project 76, the great mayors of tomorrow will occupy the vital center of American government; they will, if we are fortunate, have the authority and funds necessary to dissipate discord and to sustain and satisfy the aspirations of their people. These mayors will play a vital role in reshaping the physical city and in renovating the attitudes and practices that inhibit equal opportunity and maintain barriers between citizens. Some will be accorded that admiration and respect we now accord the best governors and United States senators. The very best of tomorrow's mayors—if there is a Project 76— will be considered by both political parties as prime candidates for President.

Project 76 would add another new dimension to American leadership. As involvement in city-building broadens and deepens, new initiatives for excellence would develop. Some who would do the most to shape the cities of tomorrow would hold no elective or appointive public offices. Their forerunners are already abroad in the land. They bear names like H. James Rouse (the creative founder-

143

developer of the new community of Columbia, Maryland) and Irwin Miller (the Columbus, Indiana, industrialist who has shown how a small, drab town can strive for and achieve distinction). Others will surely appear- `ergy-men, educators, labor leaders, designers, professionals and nonprofessionals of all sorts—to demand and contribute to the superior solutions that will remake the nation.

The new politics would also encourage neighborhood "government." Once we decide to become masters of our everyday environment, every decision, from the design of shopping areas to the location of recreation facilities, should evoke the healthy interest of affected citizens. Some of the characteristic elements of the political action of tomorrow have been foreshadowed in the national beauti-fication campaign of Mrs. Lyndon B. Johnson, which has engaged executives of huge corporations, neighborhood as-sociations, and government officials in the execution of common projects.

To achieve the paramount national goals of the past, we gave heavy subsidies to agriculture, to transportation, and to oil exploration. We must now devise a system of sub-sidies that will encourage industry to employ the latest technologies in rebuilding whole sections of cities, in eradicating slums, and in erecting attractive low-cost hous-ing interspersed throughout the urban milieu. Whether such incentives include the Kennedy-Percy proposals (spe-cial tax credits and/or special interest loans for low-income housing) or the provision of free land for developers or groups who meet new standards, we must reclaim our cities and in the process give them the same preferential treatment we have accorded agriculture for nearly two centuries.

A second, perhaps more immediately productive, form of subsidy would encourage blight removal by decisions to

144

place all new federal, state, and municipal government facilities—schools, colleges, hospitals, office buildings—at sites that would make nearby projects viable in both human and economic terms. Thus, soon after it was announced that a major New York State office building would be located in Harlem, a major hotel chain committed itself to invest in and help operate the largest private commercial venture ever undertaken in that part of Manhattan. The impact of one vast governmental installation has been demonstrated in Florida, where Cape Canaveral (now Cape Kennedy) generated the surrounding community of Cocoa Beach. In Texas, NASA's Manned Spacecraft Center resulted in the building of Clear Lake City. But smaller governmental installations can also have a favorable impact on the urban fabric, and this effect should not be ignored by these new forms of public planning.

The renewal of our politics and federal, state, and local governments can be accomplished if we seek, not so much the wholesale reconstruction of our institutions, but the sharpening of their ability to function. The question now is this: In an increasingly complex age, how can the system be made to work more efficiently and responsibly?

The answer depends on the quality of the men in the system and the ability of the system to define the nature of its tasks and to take advantage of new technologies in information storage and retrieval, computer-aided prognostication and simulation. The new technological skills will permit decision-makers to anticipate problems and to calculate better the consequences of an action in one field upon others. Computers and computer-programming techniques must become an essential decision-making tool. As former Defense Secretary Robert McNamara demonstrated so masterfully, these marvelous machines are devices that

145

can help discipline thought. If man summons the will to master his supposedly insoluble problems, properly programmed computers offer him powerful new predictive instruments and provide him with possibilities of foresight he has all too often lacked in the past.

These new tools could also open the way to the rational use of taxing policy as a device to further new national goals. Tax laws at all levels can be a determining economic factor in shaping "development" trends. Vital tax policies should be reviewed and revised to produce a framework that will encourage conservation, penalize ugliness, and stimulate those private decisions that can make America more genuinely livable. An adage of American politics is that the "power to tax is the power to destroy." In our day, the fact is that the power to tax can be the power to create. We must alter our real-property taxing policy so that it discourages the antisocial use of land and encourages its highest and best use. It is folly on the local tax level to continue to restrict the potential of education by depending solely on the real-property tax to produce operational municipal revenue. Our tax laws should reward the preservation of historic buildings (as Old San Juan in Puerto Rico already does) and give a tax break to companies that create plazas, vest-pocket parks, fountains, or other amenities. In addition, tax laws should ensure that the public recaptures the windfall created by zoning changes that confer developmental values on specific landowners. Tax-relief measures to encourage the giving of scenic easements (such as Maryland enacted to help preserve the view from George Washington's Mount Vernon) and zoning controls to encourage open-space preservation by cluster housing should also be furthered.

As we begin to employ such tools, we can make all our institutions more responsive, and bring to leadership the

146

best individuals of our land. If we rejuvenate local government as we must, our mayors might well become the creative Medicis of our society, the champions of excellence, amity, and art, the keepers of those amenities that add joy to everyday life. We must anticipate the day when the most enlightened citizens will be selected to serve as the wise leaders of their cities, gathering about them all the talent needed for the city's re-creation. The business of America must now be the business of creating communities where the good life—of equality, education, and environmental excellence—is a reality for all. But, in fact, how do we define the good life? That definition must derive from a continuing assessment of the common purpose.

At the national level there already are signs of significant positive movement: the history-changing decisions of the Supreme Court, beginning with the 1954 desegregation decision, have had a prodigious impact on our national life; and the Presidency, the most resilient office of our system, for a number of decades has been the cutting edge of the advance (except when weak Presidents have refused to use its powers). The Congress, on the other hand, has been the least adaptable, least dynamic entity of our constitutional triad. Only when its committees and individual members think and speak for the nation as a whole—and not as standpat defenders of special interests or the narrow aims of the several states—is the Congress worthy of its highest mission.

In recent years more of the Congress's finest hours have come when it was exercising over-all oversight in an attempt to help the nation resolve great issues than when it was fulfilling its bill-passing function. When it has grappled with great issues, such as during the Army-McCarthy hearings and subsequent censure debate, it has closely reflected and directly helped to change the thinking of the nation. The agonizing inquiry into the Vietnam policy conducted in March 1968 by the Senate Foreign Relations Committee and the long debate on the "new economics" further demonstrate the latent and real power of the Congress to influence the course of history. The Congress has been at its worst when it acts as the cantankerous brakeman of the *status quo* and when its response to crises can only be precipitated by such tragic events as the assassination of Dr. Martin Luther King, Jr., which brought overdue action on open-housing legislation.

The time has come for the Congress to play a more positive role in the life of the nation. To be fully effective it must modify the self-imposed shackles of its own rules. By changing the most self-limiting of its antiquated rules and procedures (most notably the rigid rule of seniority and the egregiously unconstitutional filibuster rule of the Senate), and by conferring much greater power and responsibility on the Speaker and other leaders of the Congress, our lawmakers could enlarge their capacity to lead the nation and to deal effectively with the largest issues before the nation. The inner strength of the American system of government has been an adaptability that has kept our politics reasonably abreast of change. With one notable exception (the failure to resolve the conflict that led to the Civil War) our government has met the challenges of wars and internal crises by steadily enlarging the capacity of its institutions to deal with great issues. The Congress itself can best achieve this objective today by helping the nation sharpen its sense of national priorities.

The one-man-one-vote decision of the Supreme Court and the civil-rights legislation of the 1960's, which are restoring voting rights to the disenfranchised Southern Negro, have also been vital self-renewing actions for our democracy. But to organize and perform at the tempo required by a Project 76, we will need other reforms as well.

Political renewal was central to the success of Woodrow Wilson's New Freedom and Franklin D. Roosevelt's New Deal. In their own times of tumult, new goals of national growth evolved as a consequence of a political movement whose time had come (in 1913) and as a response to a severe internal crisis (in 1933). In each case, the inadequacy of the old order and the wide gap between ideals and performance were clearly recognized. This enabled the accomplishment of such works of reconstruction and reform as the graduated income tax, statutes to control banks, trusts, and the stock market, the guarantee of labor's right to organize, the institution of Social Security and a national minimum wage, and resource programs to conserve river valleys and replant forestlands. More recently, adaptive efforts by Congress produced the reforms of 1946–47 that established the framework for a unified Department of Defense, created an Atomic Energy Commission and a Central Intelligence Agency to bolster the national security—and, within weeks after the first Soviet sputnik, established permanent space committees and initiated the U.S. space program.

It is no small scandal that a nation seventy per cent urbanized has a national legislature with no committees on urban affairs. It is equally outlandish that a nation caught in a racial conflict that imperils its future has a Congress with no committee on human relations. Washington will not develop a corps of urban experts and champions of sound city building and wise human relations until the Congress is prepared to organize itself to give these overriding issues the attention they deserve. Congress must be brought to see that it needs to give these issues the same day-to-day surveillance it accords other areas of national life.

We need aggressive, analytical, adaptive efforts more far-

149

reaching than the reforms of 1946–47, which were enacted to equip us for decision-making in the nuclear age. A proper agenda for tomorrow cannot be devised from the successes or structures of yesterday. The pressures and problems of postdepression politics left as their legacy a fragmented, reactive, narrowly program-oriented bureaucracy that dominates most of the departments of our national government. When urban failures were omnipresent, we belatedly created a Department of Housing and Urban Development; when transportation and traffic problems became unbearable, we created a Department of Transportation (two of President Lyndon Johnson's most adaptive achievements). The weakness is in our inability to view the total task of the nation. In the rush to administer its patchwork programs, the national government—and particularly the Congress—is weakest in carrying out what should be its most vital function: *the synthesis, shaping, and supervision of the nation's paramount goals and priorities.*

Governors and legislatures must necessarily deal with state problems. Mayors and their councils must wrestle with their day-to-day crises. Only the President and Congress are responsible for the nation as a whole. Yet the Congress has traditionally confined its energies to the narrow compartments of its several committees with little attention given to seeing its assorted programs in perspective or ascertaining their interrelationships. Each year while the President delivers a State of the Union address to the country and submits an annual budget that expresses Executive preferences and priorities, the Congress has been content to be a passive audience when it could readily become a vast sounding board to arouse and educate the nation. There have been occasional "great debates" on foreign policy, but few on the general welfare at home.

150

Congress has been unprepared to argue whether we are spending too much on space exploration or too little on slum renovation. The nation hears much about the President's budget and his legislative program. But we hear little about the legislative program of the legislative branch or about a Congressional budget, because neither exists. While some individual committee chairmen may have an agenda for matters within their jurisdiction, neither the Speaker of the House nor the Majority Leader of the Senate is invested with the power or the machinery to prepare an agenda for the Congress. The immense potential power of Congress is deliberately dispersed to dozens of separate and unco-ordinated power centers within the standing committees.

With no great forum to ask and answer the larger questions, we have habitually failed to relate the national purpose to national priorities. We have also failed to foresee the dangers arising from the cancer in the cities and the rising tide of racial tension. Congressional concern over the growing urban predicament might not have made us omniscient, but it could have made us aware.

We will never envision, much less build, our own Acropolis unless, for a season, we walk the high hills above the valleys of our private preoccupations. A dynamic nation requires a systematic assessment of its goals, priorities, and ideals in a public dialogue that will involve and interest every mature American.

One way to achieve this would be for the House and the Senate to sit for two or three weeks as a committee of the whole each year after the budget of the President and his State of the Union address have been presented. During this joint session Congress could undertake a searching analysis of our national performance and aspirations. It is true, of course, that national priorities are implicit in a

151

President's budget and in the assorted programs he submits from time to time to the Congress. However, most Presidents neither argue nor fully articulate these priorities, and the Congress has not in recent times seen fit to make its chambers forums for an examination of the competing demands for the financial resources of the nation.

The virtue of the committee system is that it produces expertise and concentrates microscopic attention on vital details. The defect of that virtue is that its necessarily narrow focus fragments what it scrutinizes and prevents consideration of the interrelatedness of things. The tragedy is that only consideration that unifies the entire field of action will be able to provide a sound base for building wise priorities. Analysis, by definition, is a breaking down of the whole into its constituent components. But knowledge and perspective do not emerge from the facets of fragmented subjects. They develop only by reuniting the pieces within a meaningful context.

It is my belief that an annual national assessment by the Congress would be good for both the Congress and the country. There are several possibilities for a creative staging of such a debate. The leaders of House and Senate might choose to arrange the debate and select the participants in such fashion that the leading spokesmen of both political parties were given an opportunity to think aloud for the country, to try out new ideas, to question possibly outdated assumptions, and to ask all the vital "whither are we tending" questions. The televising of this unique national "town meeting" would add a new dimension to lawmaking and enlarge the influence of the Congress. A lively and relevant exchange, using a debate format, would offer members of Congress an unprecedented opportunity to educate the country and themselves, and to produce each year a creative confrontation between the Executive and the Congress which should reinforce, not undermine, wise Presidential leadership.

In whatever form, such an assessment debate would give a resonance to Congressional deliberations which long has been lacking. It would create more contact between the Congress and the people. Moreover, there would be echoing discussions in newspapers, magazines, and in the class-rooms and living rooms of the country.

For example, had the Congress attempted to evaluate the nature and gravity of the urban crisis after the Watts section of Los Angeles was burned in the summer of 1965, decisions might have been made to stretch out the space program and invest the savings in a crash program to employ the hard-core unemployed in the ghettos. Such a debate might also have revealed that the national govern-ment was then spending vastly more money to control rodent populations invading farmers' crops than on rat-control measures to protect the health of children in slums —and the shock of this discovery might have quickly put these priorities aright.

An annual national assessment would, of itself, achieve a new and regular intimacy between the Congress and the people. As each year's goals and performance were meas-ured against those of earlier debates, public knowledge and public participation would increase, and the quality of Congressional performance would reflect it. Once Con-gressmen realized that their constituents were enlightened on vital issues, they would be better able to function with informed perspective—rather than skilled special-interest pressure—as their main guide.

As the new concepts of politics make possible the first fruits of Project 76, we might elevate our aspirations further and escalate our aims and goals. This increased awareness could become part of a feedback system now unknown in our national life.

We can rebuild our cities, reconcile our people, eliminate poverty, achieve population balance, and establish a conservation regimen that will provide a life-giving environment if we have leaders willing to propose the bold but practical steps we need to achieve these goals.

Some still argue that such Project 76 programs as are explored in this volume are beyond the reach of American politics. They are indeed beyond the limits of conventional contemporary politics, but they should not be beyond the reach of a political system capable of recovering its resiliency and its sense of mission.

Epilogue

"Some men see things as they are and say, 'Why'?
I dream things that never were and say, 'Why not'?"
—ROBERT F. KENNEDY

Is a Project 76, are the programs and new goals outlined in this book, possible? This depends on our will, on the dynamism and aspiration generated by our society, on the quickening of our capacity to correct injustice and to encourage inventive and inspired new leadership.

Our own past tells us we will not attain radiant cities unless, beyond all their physical elements, our minds encompass the foundations of a radiant social order as well. Spacious ambitions will not emerge from fragmented thinking and planning. Our ideas for cities, for conservation, and for social justice must coalesce in a single, interrelated concept. This is the classic lesson taught so cogently

155

by the ancient Greeks. Slavery subtracted from the final glory of their achievement, but the Greeks had a clear and steady vision of the cities and the society they wanted to build. They were able to transform this vision into city-states of order and beauty because they had mastered the art of interrelatedness. Edith Hamilton described their genius in simple terms: "Our way in the United States is to consider each separate theme alone by itself. The Greeks always saw things as parts of a whole." This habit of mind marked the art, architecture, and city planning of the Greeks. For their master architects, the setting of a temple or city and its relation to sea and sky and the surrounding hills was all-important. Man's needs were always dominant; design was the art of siting, of refining the proportions and scale of a single setting to make the utmost use of its gentling and civilizing potentials.

Greek civilization, to be sure, was a singular episode in man's history on earth. The Revolution of 1776 is the only episode of our history that may one day be discussed with comparable superlatives. This book is based on a faith that the fulfillment of the experiment that began in 1776 still lies in the future. A Project 76 is needed now not only that we may resolve the great issues currently confronting us, but also that we may rejuvenate American life. Can we muster the purpose and the leadership to attempt it? The answer depends on whether our society is sufficiently supple and sufficiently youthful to redefine its aims and reshape its institutions.

A vibrant society must, above all else, involve most of its citizens, and most particularly its youth, in all the exciting and demanding enterprises it undertakes. John W. Gardner has warned us that "history will judge our country harshly if it refuses to tax itself to cure its ills." I would add that the judgment will be harsher yet, and more just,

156

if we do not enlist our youth and employ our wealth to build the mature, enlightened civilization that now eludes us.

I am convinced that the American experiment will falter unless our agenda for tomorrow embraces and includes goals and purposes as spacious and ennobling as those of the Founding Fathers. We need goals that soar beyond our own selfish interests, for our most ennobling moments have come when we have acted on the faith that we owed it to mankind to exemplify and enlarge the American dream. That dream, after all, is the world's dream of peace, prosperity, freedom. To pursue it is our happiness and the health of our society.

Chapter Notes:
An Annotated List of Books

Chapter 1.   1945–1968: The Distorted Years

Two penetrating books that documented many of the serious shortcomings of what I have called "the distorted years" were John Kenneth Galbraith's *The Affluent Society* (1958) and Michael Harrington's *The Other America: Poverty in the United States* (1962). The outrage and anger of the blacks at the slow motion of "deliberate speed" progress was first made clear to most whites by James Baldwin, in *The Fire Next Time* (1963), nearly a full decade after *Brown* v. *Board of Education* shattered the shackles of the separate-but-equal doctrine. Two notable attempts to assess our national performance and priorities in the postwar years were the Rockefeller reports of 1959–60 and the "National Purpose" essays sponsored by *Life* Magazine in 1960. Yet a fresh look at the books that contained these reports—*The National Purpose* (1960) and *Prospect for America* (1961)—shows that most of our social prophets and critics misjudged the strength of the new tides surging through our society as we turned from the "normalcy" politics of the 1950's to the turmoil of the 1960's.

A recent work that gives a balanced view of the gains and achievements of the postwar United States is John Brooks's *The Great Leap* (1966). Galbraith's *The New Industrial State* (1967) is as provocative as his earlier work. For understanding the nature of our racial crisis perhaps no book is more suggestive than C. Vann Woodward's *The Strange Career of Jim Crow* (1955; rev. ed., 1966). For inspiration and pointed analysis Dr. Martin Luther King, Jr.'s *Stride Toward Freedom* (1958) and *Where Do We Go from Here: Chaos or Community?* (1967) should not be missed. There is also encouragement in the superb television documentary series "Of Black America," produced by CBS and the Xerox Corporation in 1968 and in *Climbing Jacob's Ladder* (1967), by Pat Watters and Reese Cleghorn, a thorough history of the Southern Voter Education Project.

Chapter 2. The Urban Affliction

For nearly half a century, amid all the clashing roar of "progress" and the undeniable achievements of our technology Lewis Mumford has patiently chronicled and criticized the failures and follies of mindless urbanization. His books collectively constitute a historical indictment of man's shortcomings as builders of a balanced civilization. The magisterial *The City in History* (1961) is a characteristic book. Future generations will surely wonder why Americans paid so little heed to the counsel of this trenchant critic of the impoverished social and human values that have governed our growth. See *The Urban Prospect* (1968) for Mumford's sense of current urban dilemmas.

Surprisingly few Americans have been angered by the erosion of those urban resources that form the lineaments of the great city. It is significant that the most effective phillippics against urban despoilment—such books as Jane Jacobs' *The Death and Life of Great American Cities,* Peter Blake's *God's Own Junkyard,* Richard Whalen's *A City Destroying Itself,* and Raymond Dasmann's *The Destruction of California*—have all appeared in the 1960's.

Chapter 3.   Population: Less Is More

The paucity of American writing on the impact of un-limited population expansion on the quality of life mea-sures the influence of the growth gospel, and the extent of our belief in the myth of scientific supremacy.

Fairfield Osborn's *Our Plundered Planet* (1948) is an early work that touched the fringes of this issue. William Vogt's *People! Challenge to Survival* (1960) and Harrison Brown's *The Challenge of Man's Future* (1956) explored some of the consequences of overgrowth. The "Popula-tion Crisis" hearings conducted by Senator Ernest Grue-ning during the second session of the Eighty-ninth Con-gress contain a wealth of information on virtually every aspect of this issue.

Chapter 4.   The Growth Gospel:
Some Reflections on Jefferson

Jefferson and Thoreau are, in my view, the two Ameri-can authors we can revisit most often with profit. The literature on both is immense. Jefferson's splendid exchange of letters with John Adams, written in their old age, *The Adams–Jefferson Letters* (1959), beautifully expresses his spirit and hopes. There is no more characteristic Thoreau than in *A Week on the Concord and Merrimack Rivers* (1849).

Chapter 5. Project 76: The Urban Answer

The 1960's have seen a spate of solid books inquiring into the causes and cures of our urban crisis. Some of the best are: Charles Abrams, *The City Is the Frontier* (1965); The American Institute of Architects Study, *The Potomac;* Edmund Bacon, *The Design of Cities* (1966); Kenneth B. Clark, *Dark Ghetto* (1965); Edmund Faltermayer, *Redoing America* (1968); August Heckscher, *The Public Happiness* (1962); Lawrence Halprin, *Cities* (1963); Kevin Lynch, *The Image of the City* (1960); Paul D. Spreiregen, *Urban Design: The Architecture of Towns and Cities* (1965); Christopher Tunnard and Boris Pushkarev, *Man-made America: Chaos or Control?* (1963); Wolf Von Eckardt, *A Place to Live* (1968).

The Report of the National Advisory Commission on Civil Disorders (the Kerner Commission study) laid bare the roots of our racial crisis. This report—available from the Government Printing Office in Washington and in several commercial editions—should become the bible of those concerned about real solutions to the ghetto problems. One wishes the magazines would abandon their article-by-article approach to the urban predicament and devote entire issues to this crisis as *Newsweek* did with notable results in its incisive November 20, 1967 issue entitled "The Negro in America—What Must Be Done."

A "Freedom Budget" for All Americans: Budgeting Our Resources, 1966–1975 to Achieve "Freedom from Want"

162

(A. Philip Randolph Institute, 1966) deserves close attention. Paul H. Douglas's "The Problem of Tax Loopholes," which appeared in *The American Scholar,* Winter 1967–68, and which is reprinted with other pertinent essays in his *In Our Time* (1968), discusses an urgent problem the Congress has yet to face adequately.

Chapter 6.   New Dimensions of Conservation

The *Conservation Yearbooks* of the Department of the Interior, available through the Government Printing Office, have done much to dramatize the need for the overview approach to resources, and the new sensitivity needed for their management.

John Keats's *The Insolent Chariots* (1958) is a pungent look at what the automobile has done to America and forcefully reminds us that we must grasp the interrelationships between our standard of goods and services and the preservation of our everyday environment, and therefore the various impacts of our productive and marketing decisions upon our lives.

The conservation movement needs books that inculcate a reverence for life and renew our respect for the life process itself. Loren Eiseley's reflective works on man and nature and, at another level, Teilhard de Chardin's *The Phenomenon of Man* (1959) have done much to keep the mystique of nature—and the spirit of Thoreau—alive in this country.

In addition, such hard-hitting, science-oriented books as the late Rachel Carson's *Silent Spring* (1962), George R. Stewart's *Not So Rich as You Think* (1967), Jerome B. Wiesner's *Where Science and Politics Meet* (1965), and Barry Commoner's *Science and Survival* (1966) help make the case for ecology at other, different, levels of our national life. Symposium volumes that deal with important aspects of the "new conservation" are: "Environmental Quality in a Growing Economy," published by Resources for the Future; the 1957 California Technology symposium "The Next Hundred Years" and its follow-on in 1967, "The Next Ninety Years"; the collection of articles on "America's Changing Environment" in the fall 1967 issue of *Daedalus*.

Chapter 7. Population, Parenthood, and the Quality of Life

We need writers to mine the truths science is ready to tell us about parenthood and population and their influence on the quality of life and the human equation. Jonathan Kozol's *Death at an Early Age* (1967) explores the lives of children denied a chance. *The Battered Child* (1968) by C. Henry Kempe, M.D., and Ray E. Helfer, M.D., is a shocking account of the destruction of the minds and bodies of children by parents unqualified to rear their young. Planned Parenthood—World Population has issued a number of publications to which the reader might also be directed. These include: *The Tragedy of the Unwanted Child* by Alan F. Guttmacher, M.D.; *Parenthood, Its New Responsibilities,* by Alice Day; *The Case for the Small Family,* by Winfield Best. Erik H. Erikson's *Childhood and Society* (2d ed., 1964) has already achieved the status of a contemporary classic. Kenneth Keniston's *The Uncommitted: Alienated Youth in American Society* (1965) explores the problem of disaffection and disaffiliation from our society of a group of talented and privileged young men.

Chapter 8. The Renewal of Politics

John Gardner's *Self Renewal: The Individual and the Innovative Society* (1964) contains more insights per page into the strengths and shortcomings of democratic societies than any book written in this decade. It casts light into many of the dark corners of our national life and should be read by everyone ready to contemplate a Project 76.

The role of the Congress will be crucial if city renewal is to be a reality. As an institution, the Congress is the brake of the federal government: its rules and procedures make it the instinctive ally of the *status quo.* The case for Congressional reform has been stated with clarity and vigor by Representative Richard Bolling in his *House Out of Order* (rev. ed., 1965) , and by Senator Joseph Clark in his *Congress: The Sapless Branch* (rev. ed., 1964) . The Proceedings of the Twenty-sixth American Assembly of Columbia University, entitled *The Congress and America's Future* (1965) , also are illuminating. The absence of any programmatic books by recent big-city mayors is eloquent testimony to the plight of urban America. Former Governor Terry Sanford's *Storm Over the States* (1968) is the best argument in print for the reallocation of resources to the states.

Epilogue

No book should cause us to resent more our failures as city builders—or cause us to yearn more for the superior cities and beautiful environment we could create in this country—than Edith Hamilton's classic *The Greek Way* (1930) .

165

Index

167

169